# GETTING
# THE
# BUILDERS
# IN

*If you want to know how . . .*

**Building Your Own Home**
*A practical guide to set up and manage a self-build programme
for your perfect home*

**The Beginner's Guide to Property Investment**
*The ultimate handbook for first-time buyers and would-be
property investors*

**How to be a Property Millionaire**

**The Buy-to-Let Handbook**

For full details, please send for a free copy of the
latest catalogue to:
How To Books
Spring Hill House, Spring Hill Road, Begbroke
Oxford OX5 1RX, United Kingdom
info@howtobooks.co.uk
www.howtobooks.co.uk

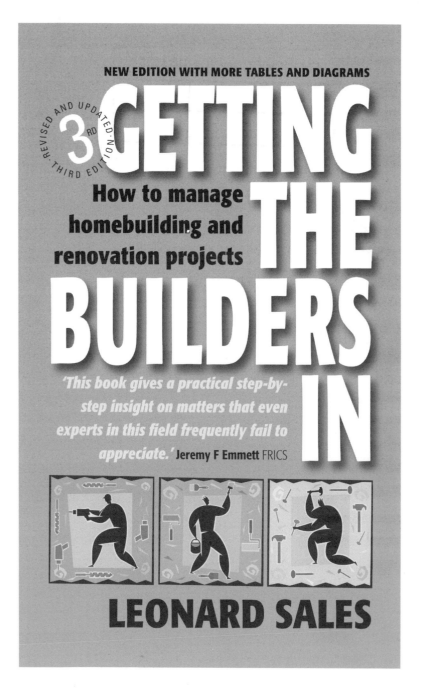

NEW EDITION WITH MORE TABLES AND DIAGRAMS

REVISED AND UPDATED · THIRD EDITION · 3RD

# GETTING THE BUILDERS IN

## How to manage homebuilding and renovation projects

'This book gives a practical step-by-step insight on matters that even experts in this field frequently fail to appreciate.' Jeremy F Emmett FRICS

# LEONARD SALES

**howto**books

Published by How To Books Ltd,
Spring Hill House, Spring Hill Road, Begbroke
Oxford OX5 1RX, United Kingdom.
Tel: (01865) 375794. Fax: (01865) 379162.
info@howtobooks.co.uk
www.howtobooks.co.uk

First published 2004
Second edition 2006
Third edition 2008

British Library Cataloguing in Publication Data
A catalogue record for this book is available from the British
Library

ISBN 978 1 84528 233 2

Cover design by Baseline Arts Ltd, Oxford
Produced for How To Books by Deer Park Productions,
Tavistock, Devon
Typeset by TW Typesetting, Plymouth, Devon
Printed and bound by Cromwell Press, Trowbridge, Wiltshire

NOTE: The material contained in this book is set out in good
faith for general guidance and no liability can be accepted for
loss or expense incurred as a result of relying in particular
circumstances on statements made in the book. The laws and
regulations are complex and liable to change, and readers
should check the current position with the relevant
authorities before making personal arrangements.

# Contents

# Introduction

## A Homebuilding and Renovating Management Book for the Uninitiated

*Congratulations!* By picking up this book you have taken the first step towards safeguarding your most important asset, *your property!* This is one book which really will help to give you 'peace of mind'.

This book is aimed at those who are planning to carry out small to medium-sized projects, it will enable you to control costs and monitor the standard of workmanship. It must be stressed, however, that each project is unique and some will require more planning than others.

Undertaking a new building project can be a daunting prospect, I have tried to cover many of the critical areas related to domestic project management in as few words as possible, avoiding long and complicated contractual jargon.

This book raises awareness of the pitfalls to avoid, the regulations to be met and the best ways to manage works from start to finish. While common sense is a necessity for any form of management, there are some procedures that require specific attention, and when it comes to construction we cannot leave anything to chance.

We hold certain professionals such as doctors and solicitors in high regard. The question is – are they always right? One reason for this level of trust we have in them is that they are for the most part regulated by their respective authoritative bodies, and they are also educated to the required level to provide the advice or services associated with their field of expertise.

In a similar way most people will rely on the word of the 'building' professionals. However, when we require advice or services from companies or people who are not regulated and who do not hold specific qualifications, we should put in place some safety precautions and procedures to ensure that we are protected, as far as practically possible.

The principles of project management that this book deals with can be applied to many different situations, the fundamentals of which we use in our daily lives, albeit subconsciously. Take, for example, buying food. Below are some of the questions we might ask and the decisions we might have to make.

- What do we need?
- When do we need it?
- How much do we need?
- Where will we get it?
- Does the supplier have a good reputation?
- How much will it cost?
- Will we buy brand names?
- Is there an alternative of the same quality but cheaper?
- Was it as good as we thought it would be?
- What was the service like?
- Would we use that supplier again?

Other situations in which these same decisions are made on a regular basis include:

- refuelling the car;
- having the car repaired;
- buying household goods;
- buying luxury items;
- buying clothes;
- planning holidays;
- buying insurance;
- buying a second-hand car.

Generally speaking, we are happy to make these decisions without too much planning, as we know the end product before we buy it. In comparison, with major building works the risks are naturally increased.

When we are planning to have work carried out in our homes, there are other factors that need to be considered. These will be covered in this book and are those elements that are unique to the domestic construction industry which we do not generally give much thought to.

Bringing these to your attention now will help you to understand the importance of reading through this book completely before moving on to the first steps of the planning stages.

Areas to take into consideration include the following:

- ◆ Your privacy:
  - ensuring areas that are off limits are secure.

- ◆ Security:
  - who will be responsible for door keys?
  - how will the builder secure holes in walls, etc.?
  - will the scaffold be alarmed?
  - who will monitor visitors?

- ◆ Safety:
  - how will excavations be made secure?

- ◆ Precautions:
  - how will rainwater be redirected?
  - what measures will be used for controlling dust, etc.?

◆ Insurance:

  – are we insured against short-term higher risks?

◆ Emergencies:

  – who do we contact in an emergency?

Despite the high level of media attention and regular stories of disasters surrounding domestic building projects, most people feel that it will not happen to them. They are prepared to risk potential difficulties, such as poor workmanship, security problems and projects running over budget and time.

Although there are many reputable builders and contractors on the domestic side of the construction industry, when the market is thriving some may exploit this situation and charge extortionate rates for carrying out substandard work.

Most of the aspects covered in this book have had volumes written about them in their own right. However, with this step-by-step approach to the fundamentals, all of these elements become easily manageable which will help to give the reader confidence in their decision-making. It will also help the client to produce the information which the builder/contractor will use to accurately price the work.

All those who use this book will learn cost-saving exercises and how to relay exactly what is required to all concerned. However, it must be stressed that, as in any form of contract, cooperation and discretion is required from all parties involved.

## Ten Golden Rules Before Starting Your Project

1. Study this book from start to finish, and pick out the elements that are suitable for the size of project that you are undertaking, and which you feel comfortable in implementing.

2. Always record agreements in writing. You may feel that you want a more legally binding contract than the examples shown in this book – your architect or legal representative should be able to organise this for you.

3. Do remember that it is your money that is being spent, so you need to be in control at all times and confident in your decision-making.

4. Set out a plan of action, study it and make changes where necessary until you are satisfied that you have covered all aspects.

5. If you feel that you are unable to project manage your own building work, do consider using a consultant. He should be able to make sufficient cost-savings to cover at least some of his fees, depending on the size of the project.

6. Do not pay money in advance unless it is for manufacturing deposits and always obtain a receipt.

7. Do remember that some builders may appear to be professional but may not perform to expectation when required.

8. Monitoring, inspecting and good communication will keep you informed and help to avoid any problems before they arise.

9. Ensure that your insurance company is aware of building works being carried out.

10. Make sure that the builder or contractor has sufficient insurance cover.

Whatever project you are preparing to undertake, planning and good contractual procedures are the key to success. I wish you every success with your project.

# About the author

**Leonard Sales ACIOB** has been in the construction industry for 31 years, having started at the age of 16 when he left school to work for his father's building company. He studied various aspects of the industry, concentrating on carpentry as his main trade.

At the age of 20 he set up his own company, working mainly in West London for selected clients on prestigious projects. However, due to the recession in the late 1980s, he had to cease trading and decided to become a site manager for a large organisation in London.

He enrolled in a professional education course in 1989, attending Chelmsford College of Further Education, and qualified for his Diploma and Certificate in Site Management in July 1992. The course of 16 modules was very comprehensive and included Project Finance and Cost Control, Contractual Procedures, Legal Responsibilities, and Health and Safety. This led to a professional qualification with the Chartered Institute of Building, a well respected world-wide organisation, which proved instrumental in obtaining positions which enabled him to work on high-profile projects in London such as the Admiralty and 10 Downing Street. He worked on a variety of other projects in the UK and overseas, including Palaces in Abu Dhabi and Saudi Arabia.

Since the early 1990s he has worked in middle and senior management for a variety of companies and has been involved in many different styles of management. He has learnt from this experience that those clients who demand the highest standards and are willing to work in conjunction with the contractor are the ones who generally get their projects finished on time and to budget. He has observed that architects generally do not want to get involved in overseeing the smaller projects as this is too time-consuming, and in most cases their services would be too expensive for the domestic client.

It is with this in mind that he has written this book for homeowners and small businesses. When used with common sense and confidence, it can assist in the smooth running of all types of projects, both large and small. Included in this book are simple-to-follow management techniques that have been used success- fully and will suit any project, whether valued at £1,000 or £1,000,000.

## (1)

# Getting Started

---

## SETTING OUT YOUR OBJECTIVES

Before starting on any kind of building work in your home or business, you need to know exactly what your objectives are, the resources that are available to you and how you are going to achieve those objectives. You also need to consider whether or not your ideas are practical and achievable within your anticipated timescales. Do remember that the planning of any work, whether it is on a large or small scale, takes time and patience.

The scale of the project will obviously dictate the amount of time required on the planning stages. If you think that your project is too small to warrant the time spent on reading all of the chapters and issues in this book, read it anyway – you may be surprised how some of the bigger issues can be scaled down to help in the smaller projects.

## SETTING OUT YOUR BUDGET

Once you are satisfied that your ideas are realistic, you

need to decide on your budget, and check you have the financial resources to carry them out.

It is important to understand that any decisions that you make in the planning stages of any home building or alteration work can have cost implications later on. These cost implications need not be to your disadvantage. If you study this book and the areas relating to cost-saving exercises, you may find that you have more to spend on your furnishings etc.

## SETTING OUT THE TECHNICAL ASPECTS

If you have little or no knowledge about the technical aspects related to your project or the logistical problems that building work involves, you will need to contact an architect or specialist designer, depending on your requirements. For example, any work that involves alterations to internal or external walls may require the advice of a structural engineer.

While builders and contractors will have had experience in carrying out the work, it is important that you satisfy yourself in the first place as to whether structural calculations and drawings will be required.

Architects' and engineers' rates vary, and can cost in excess of £80.00 per hour or a fixed fee percentage of the project. However, if you do not start off on the right track, it could cost you much more in the long run.

Obtaining outline planning approval based on basic drawings should only involve a small amount of work by the architect in comparison to a full set of detailed drawings required for full planning approval, so it is worth discussing with your architect a two stage payment scheme. If for some reason your project is not accepted you will know the initial outlay required.

Architects, engineers and designers will know what is required to obtain full planning permission and building regulation approval. If the architect has submitted drawings, calculations and any other information to the local authority in order to obtain full planning approval/consent, there may also be additional disbursement costs that you will be liable for.

It is worth obtaining estimates from the various professionals before engaging in any form of contract, as their charges can vary drastically depending on their workload. Architects and designers are market-led and in boom times may have many months' work booked in advance. They will therefore have the upper hand when negotiating fees, so be patient and shop around.

Consider speaking to friends and relatives who may have had similar work carried out on their properties, as they may be able to point you in the right direction on a number of aspects of the project.

Do remember though that it is *you* who will be employing the various professionals. You must feel comfortable about who you employ and where necessary carry out reference checks.

## MINIMISING THE INITIAL COST

You can minimise the initial costs by putting together as much information as possible. This will cut down on the amount of time the professionals would normally spend in extracting your ideas from you, and is where speaking to other people who have had similar work carried out may be of help.

It is easy enough to explain to someone what you want but, as the saying goes, 'a picture paints a thousand words'. Basic sketches can help to avoid misunderstandings and will help to avoid redrawing plans and incurring costs for abortive work. You may like ideas that you have seen in magazines or photographs – these are all visual aids that will assist in the initial concept of what you are proposing.

This will also help to speed the whole process up, as some professionals will use the design element as a pretext for taking their time to provide drawings, particularly if they have a heavy workload. Remember, though, from conception to on-site development may take more time than the building process itself – this is generally the case with small domestic projects.

## DRAWING UP A TIMETABLE

It is advisable to draw up a timetable of things to be done which will help you to keep track of the dates for issuing information, etc. It does not matter that you don't know the actual timing of some of these elements, but it will give you a format to work with which will soon become a workable programme that you can adjust as the known delivery dates become apparent.

As you can see from the sample planning programme shown in Table 1.1, by entering dates for certain elements you should start getting actual feedback from the service providers involved which will in turn help you with the adjustments required to make your planning programme more accurate.

Your service providers should be able to give you actual dates or advise you why your planned dates are not achievable. If you start off in this manner, the service providers will see that you expect the dates they supply will be realised.

| Month | JUNE | | | | JULY | AUG | SEPT | OCT |
|---|---|---|---|---|---|---|---|---|
| | Week commencing | | | | | | | |
| ACTIVITY | 2 | 9 | 16 | 23 | | | | |
| Formulate ideas and sketches | ■ | | | | | | | |
| Contact architects for quotes | | ■ | | | | | | |
| Draw up preliminary drawings | | | ■ | | | | | |
| Gain outline planning approval | | | | ■ | | | | |
| Wait for planning approval | | | | | ■ | | | |
| Draw up full specification | | | | | ■ | | | |
| Contact builders for quotes | | | | | | ■ | | |
| Assess quotes | | | | | | ■ | | |
| Negotiate and agree on quote | | | | | | ■ | | |
| Confirm contract details | | | | | | | ■ | |
| Start date | | | | | | | ■ | |
| Completion date | | | | | | | | ■ |
| Send off guarantee documents | | | | | | | | ■ |

Table 1.1 Sample planning programme

You can also see from this example that this type of pro-gramme will assist in the preparation of documents, etc.

(Note, however, that these timescales are not based on actual timings. The response times of local authorities will vary, as will those of all other service providers.)

## PROGRESS REPORTS

Do not be afraid to ask your architect or designer etc. to keep you informed of progress on a regular basis.

Unless the project has been submitted and you are awaiting approval, it would not be unreasonable to request a weekly update.

One of the most frustrating elements of home building and renovating is when you are not kept fully informed of what stage certain elements are at. This includes the input from professionals.

## INSURANCE

It should be noted that all professional consultants are required by their governing body to carry professional indemnity insurance to cover any claims made against them for failures in their services/designs. It is therefore important to have any agreement in writing and to ensure that you have read and understood the small print (if applicable). We will cover the building contractor's legal contract in Chapter 6.

Non-qualified designers (one-man bands) may be less expensive, but may not always be competent and could prove difficult or impossible to recover money from if sued. Whoever you decide to use for your professional work, ensure that you obtain or at least see a copy of their professional indemnity insurance.

## PROFESSIONAL FEES

As far as professional fees are concerned, you should look at paying around 5–15 per cent of your budget (construction costs), depending on the complexity and value of the project. You may find that in the case of a project which is technically difficult, requiring a high level of structural calculations, these percentages are exceeded.

## PLANNING PERMISSION AND SCHEME DESIGN

Once you have decided what your requirements are, and have furnished your architect/designer with sufficient information, they will produce drawings based on your ideas. These should also take into account the planning authority's criteria.

Most projects will require planning permission although minor domestic works such as porches, conservatories etc. may be approved as 'permitted development' (not requiring a planning application) by the local authority. But this should always be checked with them as the rules are complex, and it is always sensible to obtain *written* confirmation if this is the case.

### Planning guidelines

While the local authority has planning guidelines (referred to as the local plan), these are open to interpretation. Even if the planning officer is in favour of the scheme, it can often be refused by the planning committee.

Planning permission has to be obtained for most major building works. The permission deals with the issues surrounding the design, e.g. use and appearance (plans and elevation), which should not be confused with the construction drawings, e.g. sections, details, etc.

## Impact of the scheme

The planning authority will consider the general impact that the development will have on the site and surrounding area. In the case of the work being of a commercial nature, environmental issues will be considered, particularly if there are specified hazards such as dust, noise, chemicals, etc.

Not only will they consult with adjoining neighbours but they may also obtain advice/consent from other departments such as Highways, Environmental Health or other organisations such as English Heritage.

## Notification of the scheme

Part of the planning process involves notifying/advertising the development. The basic details should be advertised in the local press or by means of the 'yellow' site notice displayed on the site boundary. This allows interested parties 21 days to inspect the deposited plans and make comments to the planning departments.

## Timing of consent

Obtaining planning consent can be a lengthy process and will take at least 6–8 weeks although in practice it is more like 12–16 weeks for simple projects.

With this in mind it is, therefore, very important to consider the time of year that you would prefer to have the work carried out. If, for example, the work requires your home to be exposed to the elements and, due to financial constraints, you have decided not to have a fully covered scaffold over the property, it would make more sense to try to have the work carried out when it is less likely to be freezing cold or wet for long periods.

## Works lacking consent

It is a legal requirement to obtain planning consent (if needed) and works started without planning approval can be stopped by an injunction from the local authority. You may also incur fines, and an order to reinstate any work previously carried out appertaining to the injunction.

## Duration of consent

Normally planning permission (consent) lasts for five years. This means you have five years in which to start the work.

## BUILDING REGULATIONS

The building regulations are completely different from local authority planning approval and are concerned with the construction of the building and its services. They evolved following the Great Fire of London and were used to protect the public from dangerous building construction and to improve public hygiene, e.g. foul drainage, etc.

Due to new technology, and new and improved methods of construction, the building regulations continue to grow in size and complexity and cover most areas of construction. New areas being considered are the use of recycled building materials/products (conservation of natural resources).

Building regulations are a set of minimum requirements, which have been designed to secure the health, safety and welfare of people in and around buildings. The building regulations are made under powers given in Schedule 1 of The Building Act 1984, by the Secretary of State.

The fourteen 'parts' of Schedule 1 to the Building Act are:

A    Structure

B1    Fire Safety – Volume 1: Dwelling/Houses

B2   Fire Safety – Volume 2: Buildings other than Dwelling/Houses

C    Site preparation and resistance to contaminants and moisture

D    Toxic substances

E    Resistance to the passage of sound

F    Ventilation

G    Hygiene

H    Drainage and waste disposal

J    Combustion appliances and fuel storage systems

K    Protection from falling, collision and impact

L1A  Conservation of fuel and power – new dwellings

L1B  Conservation of fuel and power – existing dwellings

L2A  Conservation of fuel and power – new buildings other than dwellings

L2B  Conservation of fuel and power – existing buildings other than dwellings

M    Access to and use of buildings

N    Glazing – safety in relation to impact, opening and cleaning

P    Electrical safety – Dwellings

To gain a clearer understanding of these regulations for specific areas, you can access the Communities and Local Government website which can be found at www.communities.gov.uk for local and regional government including, fire, housing, planning, estate regeneration, social exclusion and neighbourhood renewal.

## Understanding your requirements

Complying with the building regulations is different from obtaining planning permission for your work. Similarly, obtaining planning permission is different from taking action to ensure that your work complies with the building regulations.

Researching details of building regulations will help you to understand what is required on your specific project. Your local authority department that deals with building control issues should be able to provide you with the information that you require. Alternatively, the department should be able to provide you with the details of where to obtain specific information.

Your architect will know which regulations are required for your project and will incorporate them in the drawings, both in writing and where necessary in detailed drawings.

## Inspection of building regulations

The regulations are inspected by BCOs (building control officers) who ensure the plans that have been approved are being followed.

It is the responsibility of the builder to inform the BCO when each of the regulations needs to be inspected. It is advisable to find out what inspections are likely to be carried out on your project, and ask the builder/contractor to provide you with written evidence that the inspection took place. The BCO may sign a visitor's book, but they will not usually sign to say that something has been inspected and passed.

This is due to the fact that, although an inspection may have been carried out and the element being inspected did not fail the inspection, there will be a final inspection at the end of the project. Elements such as drainage, glass, manholes and other aspects need to be inspected and passed once the project is complete.

The elements that need to be inspected at various stages differ but they include:

◆ excavations;
◆ foundations;
◆ membranes (damp proof courses, etc.);
◆ drainage;
◆ structural elements, etc.

### Responsibility for defective work
While the works are inspected by the BCO, it should be noted that the BCO cannot be held responsible for

defective work. The responsibility for this lies with the designer or builder.

Although the BCO must be invited to inspect the work at various stages they have no obligation to do so, and can decide to inspect elements later on in the project if they desire. This ensures that the builder/contractor is aware that at all times the work must reach the minimum standards for design and construction.

If at some stage the BCO inspects work that has been covered up such as drainage, and it subsequently fails the inspection, it will be the responsibility of the builder/contractor to rectify the work at his own expense.

### WORKS REQUIRING PLANNING PERMISSION/CONSENT

Within the domestic side of the construction industry there are five main categories of works that may require planning permission and building regulations consent (approval):

◆ extensions;
◆ loft conversions;
◆ garages;
◆ major internal alterations;
◆ major external work.

*Note:* Even replacement windows are covered by the building regulations, although some window manufacturers/suppliers are licensed to undertake these works without the need for a formal application to the local authority.

Alterations to the building structure or services require building regulation approval, although small building works can often be carried out using a 'building notice' application requiring limited information or plans. Often the building inspector will just visit the site to discuss and inspect the works.

**Extensions**
To have an extension built you will require scaled drawings. These will need to be drawn up by an architect or similar qualified person. You will need to apply for planning permission and have the approval of your local planning authority. The local planning office can be contacted via your local council offices.

As explained earlier, having drawings prepared and approved can be a long drawn-out affair so be mindful of this from the outset. From the conception of a project to actually starting work can vary from six weeks to six months, depending on its size and nature. In some cases, such as listed buildings, this may be longer and could even be rejected for a variety of reasons.

Many people set out to have an extension built expecting everything to be 100 per cent complete within four or five months. However, to ensure that everything is in place and provide room for any unforeseen circumstances, a more realistic timescale would be a minimum of seven or eight months.

### Loft conversions

Again, loft conversions will require scaled drawings which will need to meet current building regulations. You may find that there are differences in dimensions between the drawings and the finished project. This is because it is sometimes difficult to survey lofts and existing structures accurately where access is difficult or dangerous.

The person carrying out the survey for the drawing may measure the lower part of the building, i.e. room layouts, which will give a fairly precise idea of the amount of floor space available. You must remember, however, that due to the slope of the roof not all of the space will be usable for walking around and so on.

Never have a loft conversion or extension built without contacting your local authority as this work will be picked up in any surveys that are carried out when selling your property and may cause you problems. You may be required to produce calculations or 'as built' drawings, and you could even be required to return the building to its original condition.

As with extensions, you should think about allowing a minimum of seven or eight months from conception to completion, so try to have the work carried out during the driest seasons if at all possible. Trying to minimise the effect of the weather on the project could actually help to reduce any potential delays.

### Garages

You will require drawings and may need planning approval, but in most cases garages are a more straightforward affair, depending on the location and size in relation to the main building. If you are planning to build a single storey garage onto the side of your house it is worth considering increasing the foundations and design in order that you may be able to extend on top of the garage at a later date. Even if you know you will not want to extend in the future, the fact that the opportunity exists to do so may increase the selling price slightly, and may also add much more desirability for any future potential buyer.

### Internal alterations

These do not necessarily require planning approval but

for your own peace of mind it is worth enquiring with your local authority. One area of internal alterations that will require planning approval is when a single property is going to be subdivided into flats or bed-sits.

There are many issues that are raised with this type of proposal such as fire precautions and alarms, noise, access and egress, plus other issues that the regional local authority imposes. While your neighbouring property may have been subdivided, it does not mean that you will automatically obtain permission.

The local authorities may take into account elements such as how many properties have been subdivided and what impact this has had on the local environment. They will consider local schools and facilities and what effect additional cars have had on the area.

One cautionary note is that if you are planning to have two rooms knocked into one, for example, a structural engineer would be required to ensure that the correct size supports are introduced, if needed, and that the area of foundation that will be taking the distributed weights is adequate.

**External works**

There are certain regulations regarding garden walls and fencing which your local authority will advise you of. With external works you do not necessarily need precise drawings; however, a good sketch of requirements will help to avoid misunderstandings.

In order to avoid conflict with neighbours, it would be advisable to discuss your plans with them, particularly if their property is close to the work and especially if the amount of sunlight that they currently enjoy will be reduced.

Many long-running disputes with neighbours have been caused by the erection of fences which, although within the prescribed height, affect the amount of sunlight that has perhaps been enjoyed for several years before. That said, you are entitled to your privacy, but common courtesy can help to avoid misunderstandings.

Problems like this can be avoided by agreeing to erect a lower fence than you are actually allowed and having a trellis on the top section through which trailing flowers can be grown. This will allow the sunlight to still be enjoyed along with the sight of the flowers.

## TREES

If you are planning to have trees removed, you must first ensure that they do not have a tree preservation order (TPO) against them. Your local authority will advise you on this. Beware of cutting down trees that are very close to buildings as this is a major cause of subsidence. As the tree roots die off they create voids which in turn are filled by the shifting of earth around them – where the roots are extremely large this can have severe effects on foundations.

Cutting down trees with TPOs is an offence for which you can be fined. The trees on your property are your responsibility, and as such you will be expected to know what you can and cannot do. This is very important when having work carried out, in that you must ensure any such instructions not to interfere with trees are passed on to builders or contractors.

It is not widely known that many trees are protected by TPOs, which means that you need consent from the local council to carry out extensive work to them, i.e. pruning or felling. There may be other factors that need to be taken into account, particularly if you live in a conservation area. If you have any doubts at all about trees within your local environment that may be affected by your project, ensure that you make the necessary enquiries before proceeding. You should be able to obtain a copy of a free leaflet, *Protected Trees: a guide to tree preservation procedures*, from your local authority office. Remember that you can be fined for any unlawful work to trees which are protected by a TPO.

Tree preservation orders are made by a local planning authority (LPA) in order to prohibit any of the following:

- wilful damage;
- lopping;
- cutting down;
- uprooting;
- topping;
- wilful destruction.

Trees are now a more important factor of our local environment, and it is important that we appreciate them. Consent from LPAs may be necessary to carry out work to completely remove a tree, or to work on it at all. The cutting or removing of tree roots is potentially damaging and can make the tree become unstable in high winds, which would obviously pose a risk to people and property.

## MECHANICAL AND ELECTRICAL (M&E)

Most of the works considered will include mechanical or electrical elements. Known in the construction industry as mechanical and electrical, this covers all works associated with the main services:

- *mechanical* – plumbing and heating, ventilation, drainage, irrigation, gas appliances

- *electrical* – lighting and power, security alarms, audio, phones, cable TV, data cabling, etc.

Fully qualified technicians should carry out and certify all of the mechanical and electrical elements of work, whether or not they are working for a builder. It is important that they belong to a trade association such as CORGI for the mechanical work, and the NIC EIC for the electrical work.

You may have to organise some of these independently of works being undertaken by a builder, particularly with regard to the utilities and communications companies. These are the two main areas that you should be looking for certificates on completion of the project.

## LEGAL REQUIREMENTS

Apart from statutory legal requirements and insurance policies needed to start a business, individual projects may need insurance cover for the building works.

As a rule of thumb, insurance for the building works and material, etc. in *new* buildings, i.e. buildings which are not joined to an already insured property, is the responsibility of the contractor.

Works to *existing* buildings are normally covered by the client's insurance, and it is necessary for them to ensure that they notify their building insurance company prior to any work commencing. Failure to notify insurance companies may invalidate any future claim or cover (always confirm in writing or get proof of insurance). Builders should still have insurance against unforeseen mishaps.

It should never be presumed by the builder or the client that planning and building regulations approval are all that is required. If planning permission is required, confirmation of approval must be obtained in writing and stamped on any drawings.

A building lease or deeds may have restrictions that only allow you to carry out cosmetic work, and you may need to gain the freeholder's consent for any work which changes the external or internal design of the building. If in doubt consult a solicitor.

## CONDITION SCHEDULE

A condition schedule is normally associated with the letting of properties whereby the condition of walls, carpets, furniture, etc. is recorded and documented at the beginning of the agreement or let and then inspected for damage at the end of the letting period. Inspections are also carried out at specified intervals in between. If any damage is found other than those that were previously recorded and that cannot be classified as reasonable wear and tear, the tenant is responsible for the cost of remedial work.

It is therefore sensible to produce a condition schedule before you have any work carried out. If you expect builders or contractors to have regular access through the property, and in particular in areas that are not going to be worked on, the schedule would assist in identifying the level of temporary protection required. In order to protect the client's/contractor's interest, a condition schedule should be written up in order to avoid any dispute later about damage caused during the works.

Condition schedules are not restricted to internal use and can be prepared as separate or combined documents for different parts of the premises. If you plan to undertake external work only, you could draw up a condition schedule to identify existing defects and specify precautions that you would like to have put in place. You could also ask for written proposals of action the builder or contractor will take to protect your property.

After the condition schedule is prepared, it should be signed and dated by both parties to ensure that agreement of the conditions is a true reflection at the time. When the work is complete and before final payments are made, a thorough check of the items on the schedule can be carried out. If damage has been caused during the work, the damage should be repaired by the contractor at his own cost or he should make proposals to have the damage rectified if it is not within his scope.

A condition schedule may take the form of photographs or agreed lists of defects or damages that are apparent prior to the work starting. Without this agreed condition schedule the contractor may face claims for damages or be asked to repair or redecorate parts of the building or site previously damaged by others. This should be extended to cover adjoining buildings, to protect the client from claims by neighbours.

You should also take photographs of the pavement directly outside your property, as the local authority is the only organisation which can issue instructions to repair paving and kerbs that are damaged. If the damage is proved to be caused by the work to your property, you will receive the bill. It is important then that your builder/contractor is aware that he is responsible for protection for the pavement, etc.

Delivery vehicles may accidentally damage kerbs but it is very rare that they will admit to it. To ensure you are not issued with unexpected bills your builder/contractor should be aware that he is expected to control these situations and inform his suppliers in writing that they will have to pay for damage caused by their vehicles.

## PARTY WALL AWARDS

If your project involves any work to be carried out on a party wall, you may need to consult a party wall surveyor. The role of the party wall surveyor is to ensure that all regulations under the Party Wall Act 1996 are adhered to, which will of course depend on the nature and complexity of the work. The Act may affect the building owner who wishes to carry out work, or the adjoining owners who receive notification under 'the Act' of the proposed work.

Some minor works to a party wall may not necessarily require you to inform adjoining owners. However, if the planned work has the potential to cause any structural damage or to affect the strength of the wall in any way, it would be advisable to contact a qualified building professional.

Work that would be considered as minor might include:

- cutting into a party wall to repair or modify electrical recessed wiring or sockets;

- drilling into a party wall to fix shelves or pictures;

- hacking off existing plaster in order to carry out re-plastering.

The Party Wall Act provides a building owner with additional rights to carry out major work to an existing party wall. The most commonly used rights are:

- to cut into a wall to take the bearing of a beam;

- to insert a damp proof course to the full depth of the wall;

- to raise the height of the wall;

- to increase the thickness of the party wall;

- to demolish and rebuild the party wall;

- to underpin the entire thickness of a party wall;

- to protect two adjoining walls by introducing a weatherproof flashing from the higher over the lower, even if this involves cutting into an adjoining owner's independent building.

### Examples of party walls

*Party wall type A*

This is a party wall that stands astride the boundary of land belonging to two owners or more.

A wall is a party fence wall if it is not part of any building but stands astride the boundary line that consists of lands of different owners, i.e. garden wall, but not wooden or garden fences.

An illustration is shown in Figure 1.2.

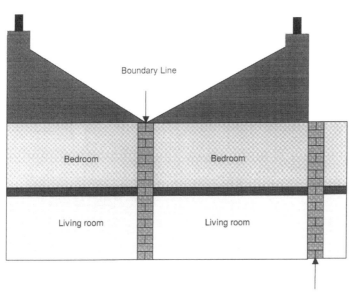

Figure 1.2 Party wall type A

*Party wall type B*

This is a party wall which stands completely on one owner's land, but is used by an adjoining owner to separate their buildings.

This could be where one person has abutted their building against an existing wall.

An illustration is shown in Figure 1.3.

*Party structure*

The Act also covers party structures which are floor partitions separating buildings or parts of buildings approached by separate staircases or entrances. This

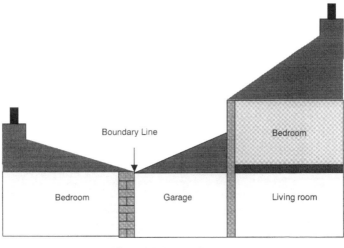

Figure 1.3 Party wall type B

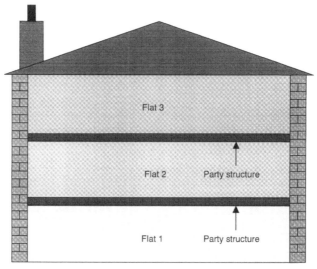

Figure 1.4 Party structure

term is used in structures such as flats or multiple properties within one building.

An illustration is shown in Figure 1.4.

## Requirements for major work

If you intend to carry out major works to a party wall, you are obliged to inform all adjoining owners two months or more before starting the work. If the adjoining owner is agreeable, you may be allowed to start the work. The work notice is only valid for one year, so it is important not to serve it too soon. You must inform or give notice to the adjoining owners about your intentions to cut into your own side of the wall to carry out any part of a major element of work. The Act allows for such types of work as:

- load bearing onto party walls – extensive renovation projects that are going to be carried out directly to an existing party wall or structure;

- new building at or astride the boundary line between properties;

- depending on the depth of a proposed hole or foundations, excavations within 3 or 6 metres of a neighbouring building or structure.

Reaching an agreement with the adjoining owner for your work does not remove the possible need to apply for planning permission. You will also need to keep your work to the standards and approval of the building regulations procedures. If your work falls within the Act you are legally obliged to notify adjoining owners. The type of work falling within the Act would include:

◆ work on an existing structure or wall that is shared with an adjoining owner;

◆ building a wall up to or astride the boundary with a neighbouring property;

◆ building a free standing wall astride the boundary with a neighbouring property;

◆ excavating near a neighbouring building.

### Disputes

The Act provides a process for preventing and resolving disputes in relation to party walls.

Where an agreement has not been made or if there is no written consent, the Act provides for the resolution of disputes arising from these situations.

## ISSUING A NOTICE

You may issue a notice to the adjoining owner in person, or by post. If the neighbouring property is empty you may address the notice to The Owner, fixing it to a conspicuous part of the premises. You are not obliged to inform the local authority of your notice.

As there is no official form for issuing a notice, you must write in person and include the following details:

♦ your own name and address;

♦ the name and address of any joint owners;

♦ the full address of the building where the work will be carried out;

♦ details of the proposed work including drawings where appropriate;

♦ the proposed start date (which must not be before the notice period of two months) as required under the Act;

♦ the date.

It should be made clear that the letter is a notice under the provisions of the Party Wall Act.

There are no enforcement procedures for failure to inform or serve a notice on an adjoining owner. It must be stressed, however, that if you did undertake work without issuing a notice, the adjoining owners have rights to stop your work through a court injunction or to seek other legal action.

Adjoining owners cannot stop anyone from exercising their rights under the Act, although they may be given opportunities to influence the methods used for the work. This could affect the timing of the proposed work.

The process for dealing with party wall issues can be long and arduous – it is therefore important to seek to reach a mutually agreeable arrangement.

$$\textbf{2}$$

# Know Your Requirements

## DRAWING UP A SPECIFICATION

The specification is a detailed description of the materials that will be used and should be written in such a way that there is no room for misunderstanding. Most cost increases arise from changes to the design and specifications and/or clarification of inadequate specifications.

If a builder or contractor is left to carry out work from a specification that is loosely written and his interpretation does not match your expectations, you may find that disagreements start to cloud the client–contractor relationship early on in the project.

It is therefore very important that you list all of the elements that you know will form each part of the works, and then break these elements down to ensure that they will meet your expectations of the finished product. As you will see from the sample specification in Table 2.1, each element of work can be separated

| Sample Specification | | |
|---|---|---|
| Element | Details | Dimensions |
| Bricks | London stocks, mortar to match existing (sample for approval required) | 215 × 100 |
| Blocks | Lightweight Celcon | 100 × 440 |
| Roof structure | As per drawing, open cut roof (see structural drawing for dims) all timber to be pretreated | |
| Roof tiles | To match existing, clay tiles | 250 × 150 |
| Rainwater goods | To match existing, cast iron | 110 × 55 |
| Windows | New uPVC windows as sample with lead lights | |
| Internal walls | All walls to be timber studs, all timber to be pretreated, 12.5 mm plasterboard and skim coat | 100 × 50 |
| Heating system | New boiler and new 'period' cast iron radiators | |
| Electrical system | New electrical system as per drawing, all faceplates and fittings to be supplied by client | |
| TV & phone points | As per drawing, faceplates supplied by client | |
| Carpentry | Skirting to be Torus (150 × 25) architrave Torus (75 × 25) softwood doors and frames, doors to be six-panel to match existing. Brass ironmongery (supplied by client) | |
| Window sills | Softwood pine | 200 × 32 |
| Wall finishes | Three coats white vinyl silk emulsion | |
| Ceiling finish | Three coats white matt emulsion | |
| Finish on bare wood | Three coats light stain as supplied by client | |
| Kitchen units | Supplied by client, builder to fit only | |
| Wall tiles | Supplied by client, builder to fix only using waterproof adhesive and grout | 150 × 150 |
| Floor finishes | Builder to supply adhesive and grout for laying stone floor tiles in kitchen (tiles supplied by client) | |
| Carpets | Client to arrange, supply and fit on completion of works | |
| Curtain rails | Pine rails to be fixed to each window | 100 × 25 |
| External work | Lay slabs to areas as detailed on drawing, all to specification on drawing | |

Table 2.1 Sample specification

and dealt with individually. This will help to avoid any potential misunderstanding.

You can also treat each room as an individual element, and in fact it is advisable to do so particularly if your colour scheme or finishings are different from other rooms. If you are only having internal alterations carried out, ensure that at the very least you have a plan of each floor in order to name each room. Remember that each bedroom must be specifically named, i.e. bedroom 1, 2, 3, etc. to ensure that mistakes are not made.

The completed specification may be included on the drawing. However, it is normally issued as a separate document. The work can, therefore, be priced in detail which will enable you to make cost savings where required.

It is worth taking the time to cover as much as possible in the specification as this will be an important factor when obtaining quotes. The more detailed information you can provide, the more the builders/contractors can price on a 'like for like' basis, which allows you to judge fairly between quotations.

## Estimates

If you are on a tight budget, do not accept an estimate that is all encompassing. If you need the estimate to show where you can make savings by reducing the amount of work, ask the builder/contractor to provide a breakdown of his estimate.

If you do request a breakdown estimate for the specification, you must bear in mind that overheads, running costs and profit are built into the rates and some figures may appear to be high when in fact they may be very reasonable. This is where obtaining several quotes will help you to understand how each company builds up their quote.

**Making cost savings**

There are regulations that govern the standard and quality of some of the materials that will be used, such as underground drainage, insulation material, glass, fire resisting material, etc. There are, however, cost savings that can be made by using alternative materials. This is something that you will need to discuss with your builder or material supplier, but ultimately the material *must* comply with the building regulations.

If you notice material changes from that in the specification, particularly material which will eventually be covered up such as floorboards or pipework, speak to your builder about it. He may be making cost savings at your expense!

When it comes to the finishes you must ensure that it is *your* specification that is being worked to and is specific to *your* requirements. Your local building material supplier and associated suppliers will normally be happy to assist in advising on the appropriate materials for given situations. Do not be afraid to ask.

## Breakdown of the specification

As you can see, the specification has an important part to play in detailing the overall building specification. This can be broken down even further by producing finishing schedules for specific elements such as:

- decoration finishes;
- floor finishes;
- ironmongery details.

Examples of these are shown in tables 2.2, 2.3 and 2.4.

| Sample Room Finishing Schedule: Bedroom 1 | | | | | | | |
|---|---|---|---|---|---|---|---|
| Element | Paint | Stain | Matt | Vinyl | Eggshell | Tile | Paper |
| 1  Doors | | × | | | | | |
| 3  Wall finishes | × | | | × | | | |
| 4  Ceiling finishes | × | | × | | | | |
| 6  Skirting | | × | | | | | |
| 7  Architrave | | × | | | | | |

Table 2.2 Sample decoration finishes

| Sample Floor Finishing Schedule | | | | |
|---|---|---|---|---|
| Room | Floor boards stained | Carpet | Tiles | Vinyl |
| 1  Hall/stairs/landing | Yes | | | |
| 2  Living room | Yes | | | |
| 3  Dining room | Yes | | | |
| 4  Kitchen | | | Yes | |
| 5  Study | | Yes | | |
| 6  Downstairs w/c | | | | Yes |
| 7  Bedroom 1 | | Yes | | |
| 8  Bedroom 2 | | Yes | | |
| 9  Bedroom 3 | | Yes | | |
| 10  En suite Bedroom 1 | | | Yes | |
| 11  Family bathroom w/c | | | Yes | |
| 12  Shower room | | | Yes | |

Table 2.3 Sample floor finishes

| Sample Ironmongery Details | | | | | | | | | |
|---|---|---|---|---|---|---|---|---|---|
| Door number | Hinges | Knobs & latches | 5 lever dead lock | 150 mm slide bolt | Yale | Letter plate | Security bolt | Brass |
| 1  DG 01 | 3 × 100 mm | | Yes | Yes × 2 | Yes | Yes | Yes × 2 | Yes |
| 2  DG 02 | 2 × 100 mm | Yes | | | | | | Yes |
| 3  DG 03 | 2 × 100 mm | Yes | | | | | Yes × 2 | Yes |
| 4  DG 04 | 2 × 100 mm | Yes | | | | | | Yes |
| 5  DG 05 | 3 × 100 mm | Yes | Yes | Yes × 2 | | | Yes × 2 | Yes |
| 6  D1 01 | 2 × 100 mm | Yes | | | | | | Yes |
| 7  D1 02 | 2 × 100 mm | Yes | | | | | | Yes |
| 8  D1 03 | 2 × 100 mm | Yes | | | | | Yes × 2 | Yes |
| 9  D1 04 | 2 × 100 mm | Yes | | | | | | Yes |
| 10  D1 05 | 2 × 100 mm | Yes | | | | | | Yes |
| 11  D1 06 | 2 × 100 mm | Yes | | | | | | Yes |
| 12  D1 07 | 2 × 100 mm | Yes | | | | | | Yes |

Table 2.4 Sample ironmongery details

## Changes to the specification

Although you may prepare a comprehensive specification, if the property is old and there is limited historic information, you may find that there are circumstances that require you to change the specification or to instruct additional work to be carried out to meet building regulations.

One example of this is where a party wall in the roof space does not meet the fire regulations. Another is where asbestos is encountered, which would require removal and disposal by specialist contractors once the proper tests have been carried out to ascertain the type of asbestos found.

Further common problems in older properties are dry rot and wet rot, two conditions which can have serious consequences on the cost and timing of a project. It is worth considering having a full survey carried out by a specialist if you are in any doubt.

If you are considering having new roof tiles and your existing tiles are slate, you need to ensure that the type of tile that you have chosen does not exceed the weight of the tiles that are being replaced.

This is particularly important on older properties where the rafters may be smaller. You should always ensure that if heavier tiles are being fixed in place of the existing slates, additional supports have been introduced to spread the additional weight to the appropriate supporting walls.

Always remember that if you decide to change the specification on site for any reason, it may affect the eventual cost of the project. Be sure that you know the consequences of changes before you make them wherever possible.

Changes to the specification can sometimes be incorporated in the original quote. However, where there is a material change, costs may be incurred due to the duration of the project being extended, even if the material is the same price. Restocking of material and revised delivery times come at a price.

**Data cabling**

Even if *you* do not require data cabling facilities to be installed, it is worth considering having the cables put in with the electrical system, as many people are now working from home and this may be an advantage when selling the property. With the advance of technology growing at a rapid pace and the cost of hi-tech equipment becoming more affordable, you may decide to take advantage of this in the future.

Data cabling can be terminated in wall sockets that are similar to telephone sockets. These allow complex systems to be installed which will enable the control of audio systems and the operation of any other remotely accessible equipment from any room in the house.

## Installing security measures

Another area that most people are concerned about is security – the possibility of burglars entering their property. This is an area that seems to be of high priority in the mind, but is one that is put off until a later date as it is mistakenly thought that intruder alarms are expensive. In reality, alarms give peace of mind and can pay for themselves in a short space of time, as insurance companies will normally reduce the premiums when alarms are fitted.

This may also be the case if you have a range of window and door locks fitted that meet the insurer's requirements for 'adequate security provisions'.

If the installation of a security alarm does not fit in with your budget, it is worth installing the cables while floorboards are up or where other cables are being run. You then have the option of installing the necessary equipment at a later date. Even if you do not have technical equipment or alarms installed, it may make a difference to the desirability when selling the property, and may even add to the selling price.

### Certification

All building works which include plumbing, heating and electrical work must meet certain regulations which will require certification.

## SECURITY ON SITE

This is an area that does not usually have enough attention paid to it by builders in general and is something that can be overlooked by the client. When you employ the services of a builder or contractor you would naturally assume that he has thought about site security and weather protection. This is not always the case and when things go wrong in this department it can sour relations severely.

If there is any doubt about the security that is being provided, most insurance companies will use this to avoid making payment on claims for theft or damage. Most building work will entail the need for workers to have access to parts of the main building on a regular basis. You must therefore take all precautions to avoid any unforeseen problems. This is explained in Chapter 7 under Method Statements.

## HEALTH AND SAFETY ON SITE

There are particular health and safety regulations for the construction industry which are very comprehensive. Your builder should be aware of these regulations. However, the domestic side of the construction industry is not regulated to the extent that it should be. Nevertheless, domestic builders are beginning to understand that they have a responsibility to you as a client and their own employees with regard to health and safety.

When you employ the services of a builder in a building you intend to use as your residential home, you are undertaking a moral health and safety obligation. Understanding the importance of health & safety is something that cannot be ignored. Any person who has contact with the project has a right under health and safety law to be protected from danger.

If you are going to employ individual contractors to carry out the work (for example, carpentry), they should have their own public liability insurance and work to good building practices. All necessary measures should be taken to remove or reduce the risks of accident by introducing methods of controlling the risk.

When you consider employing the services of individual contractors or a main contractor, it is important to satisfy yourself that they are competent and can work safely. If you are responsible for the site and a person is injured due to negligence on your part, they could take legal action against you.

If you are in any doubt about the health and safety precautions or procedures that you need to consider, contact the Health and Safety Executive helpline on 0845 3450055. Alternatively you can obtain information from the HSE website: www.hse.gov.uk.

### Personal protective equipment

One important element to pay attention to is the use of personal protective equipment (PPE). PPE is inexpensive and should be used in conjunction with other control methods. The use of basic PPE such as hard hats, masks, goggles and gloves, is all too often ignored in the domestic side of the construction industry.

It is important to select and use the right type of equipment. Your local PPE supplier should be able to help you identify your exact requirements. Plant hire shops will usually provide some of this equipment as part of their service.

PPE that you would expect to see on a construction site of any nature could include:

◆ hard hat;

◆ goggles (specifically for grinding or cutting with a disc cutter);

- ear defenders;

- ear plugs;

- masks (lightweight for general dusty work);

- masks (rubber with a filter canister for gas emissions or paint fumes);

- gloves (heavy duty cotton or rubber);

- knee protectors;

- safety glasses (for general use with circular saws, etc.);

- steel toe cap boots;

- high-visibility jacket.

As you can see from this list, there are many items of PPE that you may require but it is unlikely that you will need them all.

**Welfare**

Workplace safety covers a wide range including the provision of welfare facilities. Contractors have a legal obligation to their workforce and the following are some of the issues that need to be considered on all sites:

- maintaining the internal working environment:
  – ventilation

- heating (subject to the nature of work and common sense)
- lighting;

◆ where the work involves motorised plant, managing the movement of vehicles and pedestrians in the workplace;

◆ preventing falls from height;

◆ preventing people being struck by falling objects;

◆ providing a safe workplace;

◆ providing and maintaining the equipment in a safe condition;

◆ providing adequate welfare facilities such as sanitary and washing facilities (although shared facilities can be negotiated, and would be usual on small projects);

◆ ensuring safety when storing or stacking materials.

The condition of a building is often a major contributing factor where accidents occur. Most accidents that occur in the workplace are generally due to slips, trips and falls – these accidents are easily prevented. Working at heights and working near vehicle movements will need to be very well controlled in order to avoid serious injuries or fatalities.

Employers or individuals who are in control of a building site should always carry out risk assessments on the work activities being undertaken to ensure that proper control measures are in place.

**Checklist for health and safety considerations**

- **Signage:**
  - Externally

    Are pedestrians and neighbours adequately informed of potential dangers?

    Are signs in the correct positions?
  - On site

    Are sufficient signs placed in prominent positions for visitors and site personnel to comply with?

- **Personal Protective Equipment:**
  - Storage

    Are the right facilities available for storing PPE?
  - Provision

    Do you have the correct PPE?
  - Use

    Are you and the site personnel using it?

- **Site rules for:**
  - Site personnel
  - Contractors

- **First aid:**
  - Information

Do you have provisions on site?

Do you know who will provide first aid if required?

– Equipment

Is the appropriate equipment on site?

Under the Health and Safety at Work Act 1974, employers have statutory obligations to adhere to. These obligations are based upon common law principles. The effect of the Act has been to bring *all* people at work (and others) under the protection of the law. The Act covers all employment activities and applies to employers, self-employed persons, subcontractors, visitors to places of employment, employees, directors and managers, members of the public, designers, suppliers, etc. It also provides the Health and Safety Executive (HSE) with various enforcement powers.

### General duties

All work activities that pose a high risk to employees or other people require a correspondingly high degree of effort to ensure that those risks are controlled. Similarly, those that pose a low risk should require a lesser degree of effort and time to control.

Some duties are absolute, and an employer *must* comply.

Other duties are qualified by terms such as 'so far as is reasonably practicable', 'so far as is practicable' and 'best practicable means'. These standards rely upon the courts for interpretation. 'So far as is reasonably practicable' means that the degree of risk must be balanced against the cost necessary to combat it.

The builder/contractor or his representative must firstly identify and assess the risk, its severity, the frequency of exposure to the risk or duration of exposure, and the number of people who could be affected.

The cost of doing something about the risk then needs to be calculated. Cost is not just measured in monetary terms but also in time, effort and degree of difficulty. Most employers find that time represents the largest cost.

### Safety policy

Where a builder/contractor employs five or more people, he must provide and revise as appropriate a written safety policy. The safety policy must contain:

◆ a general statement of the employer's general policy with respect to health and safety;

◆ the organisation and arrangements that exist for carrying out that policy.

The policy and any revision must be brought to the attention of the employees.

Do not be afraid to ask a potential builder for his safety policy. If he readily agrees to this and you find yourself with the document within a day or two, the chances are he has a professional approach to his work. If, however, he does not know what you are talking about, it does not necessarily mean that he is not capable of carrying out his work safely.

However, it is important to let him know that you expect full consideration in this respect, and that you would like to see some evidence of how he plans to meet his health and safety obligations. If you get nothing at all from him, it is unlikely that he takes the issue as seriously as he should.

**Inspection of other sites**

If your project is of a significant size, it is worth visiting property which is currently being worked on by any builders that you may be considering using before engaging in any contract. This will enable you to see how they operate, the cleanliness of the site, etc. If you feel that you would like to know more, it would not be unreasonable to ask the property owners if they have any objection to discussing their satisfaction with the builder/contractor.

One point to remember when inspecting any site is that a clean site is generally a safe site and would indicate an organised foreman or site manager at the very least. If during the project you can see that the standard of health and safety is very poor, you need to stop the project and ensure that before the work continues the senior manager has satisfied you with his proposals to address the situation.

# 3

# Contacting Contractors

## CONTRACTORS AND THE SIZE OF THE PROJECT

It is important to understand that while individual builders/contractors are generally capable of undertaking projects within their experience, capability and financial scope, many builders/contractors will not turn work away even if they have a full order book. When this occurs they end up trying to keep everybody happy, and if they do not have the resources to cope with the additional workload, it is the client who is let down.

This is an important factor with regard to cash flow as the more work the builder/contractor takes on, the more he will have to pay out, and this can be very difficult on the larger projects as it is the builder/contractor who will be expected to finance the initial stages.

He can expect to receive payments in arrears by up to two months on larger projects. If possible, it is worth finding out the size of projects that the builder/contractor takes on. Don't just take his word for it –

ask for information on recent projects of a similar size to yours.

You need to make any potential contractor aware of your estimated budget and that you will be making stage payments. This is covered in Chapter 7.

## DIRECTORIES

One place to start the search for a contractor is a telephone directory such as the *Yellow Pages*. This is particularly useful as the more professional builder will normally belong to one of the major trade associations and will show their logo on the advert. This does not mean to say that they are better, just that they are prepared to have information about themselves available from a third party, which would indicate that they are confident in their own service.

## LOCAL PAPERS

Small one-man operation builders generally advertise in this way and provide a service for the smaller projects. However, it would generally be fair to say that the larger and more professional the advert, the larger and more professional the company.

## RECOMMENDATION

Most people know someone who has had work carried out. This is probably one of the most reassuring ways of finding a reliable builder/contractor, as you can discover first-hand if there were any problems. This method may even give you an opportunity to inspect the work that they carried out, to see the quality of workmanship.

You may also know someone who is currently having work done. You will get no better feel for a company than actually seeing how they operate and how the men treat the client's premises!

Although we are concerned about whether or not the builder/contractor is capable of carrying out the work, it is advisable to meet the person that you may be entering into a contract with, as you need to be sure that you will get along with that person generally.

You would not necessarily exclude a builder/contractor just because you did not like the look of him. However, a person's attitude generally can give a good indication to their work attitude. This is something that also needs to be taken into account with his employees.

It is worth mentioning at this point that if you do have problems with any of the employees on site, you should take this up with the builder/contractor himself rather than get into confrontation with the particular individuals.

## ADVERTISING BOARDS

Builders who are prepared to put a board outside a job or who advertise on their vans are in the main confident in their work. As you travel around you will see many signs of work being carried out.

Take a good look at the cleanliness of the site and note whether the area is tidy. If you get the opportunity, stop and ask to see the person in charge. This will give you a much better chance to see the site set-up and if they work in a professional manner.

## THE INTERNET

If you have access to the Internet, you can search many different internet directories to find local builders who may even have their own website. This will allow you to find out much more about the nature of projects that they undertake and how they operate in advance of contacting them.

Their website may also have pictures of work that they have carried out which will give you an indication of the size of projects that they can cope with. It would be fair to say that companies who do have their own website are, again, confident that the service that they are supplying is of a high standard, and that they should have a fairly good system in place for providing computer-assisted letters and contractual information which is always important.

## THE RESPONSE TO YOUR ENQUIRY

Depending on market forces, you may find that you get an initial favourable response, with builders/contractors coming to see you about your enquiry. However, it is a fact that, due to other work commitments, many contractors do not respond as quickly as clients would like.

In many cases they may not respond at all if it is a project that they are not particularly interested in. For this reason, it is important for you to know the type of work that a particular builder/contractor will or will not be interested in.

Even if a builder/contractor does carry out the type of work that you are trying to obtain quotes for, they will not necessarily tell you if they are not interested. It is worth seeking quotes from six or seven outfits, of which three may actually respond. Even then you may be able to tell who is submitting a quote but does not necessarily want to win the contract, by the vast difference in price.

Unfortunately some contractors will submit quotes that may be as much as 50 per cent above the going rate, if they already have too much work to cope with. If they are then awarded the contract, they will possibly use another contractor to carry out the work, or they will juggle their workforce around to do the work because of the high mark-up.

The problem with this arrangement is that the builder/ contractor may be spreading his men around too thinly and not supplying a good service to anyone, as mentioned above. On the other hand, if he does use another contractor, this could become complicated if things start to go wrong.

Builders have also been known to price projects high in order to lose them for reasons such as difficulty with parking, or a terraced property with difficult rear access.

Finally do not wait to see what response you get – be prepared to chase the quote. Remember that builders generally have to plan their work well in advance and may have order books as long as six months or more.

## Quotes and estimates

When you do receive a quote/estimate, be sure to have the builder/contractor confirm to you in writing that it is a 'quote' he is prepared to stand by. Some builders/ contractors have been known to give a client an 'estimate' knowing that the work cannot possibly be carried out for the figure that they have submitted. Their way out of this is to say that it was an estimate and not a quote!

In theory they are correct, and court cases have been won by builders/contractors who have proved that, because they worded the price of the project in a specific way, the client should pay the additional costs. Obviously if the situation gets to this stage, relations are normally irretrievable and the client could end up paying compensation on top.

Although these are extreme situations, they are worth bearing in mind.

# 4

# Establishing Credibility

## REFERENCE CHECKS

Whichever method you have used to find a builder/
contractor, it is advisable to satisfy yourself that he is
capable of carrying out the works to the standards that
you expect and that he is in a position to finance the
initial stages of the work. If the contractor has not
come via recommendation, ask him if he has any
objection to showing you projects of a similar size
which he has carried out.

You could ask the builder/contractor for written
references from satisfied customers and for contact
numbers for taking up references from other sources,
such as suppliers.

In addition, there are agencies that you can contact to
carry out credit checks, which you may decide to use
if you feel that your chosen builder may not be in a
position to finance the initial stages of the project.
Your bank may be able to advise you on the best
course of action in this regard.

One thing to bear in mind when carrying out reference checks is that if you do not find out anything about your choice of builder/contractor, and the project did get into difficulties which subsequently meant that the builder/contractor was unable to complete the project, the next builder would be likely to charge more than the going rate to take over, and would be justified in doing so.

This is due to the fact that he will need to inspect the work that has been carried out, to ensure that all of the material installed complies with the building regulations and conforms to health and safety requirements.

Depending on the nature and reason for the change of builder/contractor, the new contractor may have to remove works that have not been installed to the correct standard. This may have obvious additional financial consequences. He may even have to interrupt his scheduled work or employ labour at short notice from agencies, which would also incur additional costs.

## PORTFOLIOS OF WORK COMPLETED

Builders/contractors with a comprehensive photographic portfolio are generally client-orientated and only too willing to help with design input to finishes. If you are not very good with interior design, remember that builders/contractors by the very nature of their work are constantly working on other people's property and may be able to offer good ideas and advice.

In fact, this is also a good opportunity to ask to see some samples of work that the builder/contractor has carried out for other clients. Go to see the work itself – most people would not object to this, particularly if the project was satisfactorily completed within time and budget.

*Note*: Most building projects rarely finish on time and budget. However, there are usually justifiable reasons for this, which is where good project management and record keeping is the key to successfully completed projects.

## INSPECTING THE COMPANY SET-UP

It is worth taking the time and effort to visit the prospective builder/contractor's office set-up as this will give you some idea of his professionalism. If you find that his office and yard are messy, this may indicate how he operates on site – it would be fair to say that people whose own office, yard or home are very tidy and organised would be more inclined to operate on site in a similar fashion.

You will find that by taking the time to carry out these checks, you will get an understanding of the contractor's capabilities. This will help in your decision-making when you come to choose who will carry out the work.

## ESTABLISHING INSURANCE COVER

Most reputable builders/contractors will have adequate insurance cover. However, it is important that they confirm to you that they do so.

The types of insurance cover that the builder/contractor should have are:

♦ employer's liability – this is a good indication of responsibility;

♦ public liability – it is advisable to insist on this;

♦ contracts works cover – this is a must.

### Employer's liability

The Employer's Liability (Compulsory Insurance) Act 1969 requires all employers (with limited exceptions) to maintain insurance cover for their own potential liability to employees. There have been some changes to this Act, which was brought into effect from 1 January 1972, with, for example, the minimum amount of cover being raised from £1m to £5m in 1999.

## Public liability

Public liability insurance is important, as this will cover any persons who are injured during any building works as a result of the act or negligence of the builder/ contractor.

## Contracts work cover

Contracts work cover or similar is also very important, as any damage caused to your property will be rectified at the expense of the builder/contractor's insurance and not yours. Types of damage could include inadequate weather protection or negligent work methods leading to damage, fire, flooding, etc.

## Requirements of your own insurance

It is advisable to contact your own insurance company to ascertain what is needed, as there may be a clause in your own insurance policy that requires particular types of insurance to be provided by the builder/ contractor before he carries out any work on your property.

Your own insurance may be invalidated if you do not inform your insurance company of any building works being undertaken, particularly where scaffolding or excavations are involved. Your insurance company may ask you to provide copies of the relevant policies held by the contractor.

Needless to say, it is advisable *not* to allow any building work to be carried out by uninsured builders/contractors.

## INSPECTION OF EQUIPMENT

When carrying out any visual inspection of sites or projects being undertaken by potential builders/contractors, it is worth taking note of the condition of the equipment that is being used.

If the equipment is old and rusty, or if there are electrical leads running on the ground, this would give an indication of poor standards of work and health and safety.

As a rule of thumb, sites that not only look clean and tidy but also use bright clean equipment would indicate good standards all round. If hired equipment is being used, it may not mean that the builder/contractor can't afford it but that hired equipment is usually very well maintained and storage facilities are not required.

If the builder/contractor is using 240 V power and has 240 V leads running around the site, he is putting everyone involved in the project at risk. Sites are required to use only 110 V equipment.

# 5

# Obtaining and Agreeing Quotes

## 'LIKE FOR LIKE' QUOTES

Before you even consider who you will be inviting to tender for your project, it is important to understand that in order for you to compare competitive quotes, the contractors must be given a copy of the same drawings and specification and any other supporting documents, such as engineer's calculations or mechanical and electrical information.

Most projects will require the contractor to carry out their own measurements and inspections. These may bring to light elements that have not been included in the specification.

At the very least you should expect the builder/contractor to visit the property to see for himself where the property and therefore the work will be carried out. If they do pick up elements that have not been detailed, ensure that these form part of the written quote.

By visiting the property the builder/contractor will be able to assess any potential logistical or other problems that may exist, such as parking restrictions, narrow roads, lack of material storage space and so on.

## BREAKDOWN OF QUOTE

When inviting builders/contractors to quote, ask them to break down the quote to the elements in the specification. This is a good way to help you make cost savings either by reducing the specification or by removing some elements completely.

As you can see in the sample specification provided in Chapter 2 (see Table 2.1), the work is broken down into various elements. Although you may meet some resistance when requesting a breakdown quote, it is clear that the work can only be quoted for properly if all of the material and labour have been measured against the drawings and specification.

The quality of information that you provide should be reflected in the information that you receive back from builders or contractors. You will need to at least provide a breakdown of the elements in the project. This information could simply identify the elements that need to be priced. The sheet could indicate what you will be responsible for providing or undertaking yourself.

If you are presented with a quote that is considerably cheaper than others, it may be that the company or person providing the quote has lower overheads or has a lower profit margin. It would be sensible for you to make detailed enquiries into how the price has been put together. You must be satisfied that the project or task that has been quoted for, can be completed satisfactorily within the price. If you do not feel confident in the ability of a company or person, it would be advisable to consider carefully whether to enter into a contract with them.

It is in your and the contractors' interest to know the true cost, as you may be surprised and find that the quote has come in under your budget, which would leave you to either upgrade the specification or have other work carried out.

The elements of the specification can also form the basis for the programme of works.

**Mistakes in a quote**

If a builder or contractor has made a mistake in a quote that has been accepted, he may try to find ways to increase the costs. This situation has the potential to cause problems as the client would have accepted the quote in good faith. Even where a legal contract is in place, builders and contractors will try to find ways to keep the costs down if they have underpriced a job.

If a builder or contractor stands to lose too much money by keeping to their commitment, they may try to use inferior labour or materials to save money. If they are owed a considerable amount, the likelihood of them pulling out of the contract would be limited. If a genuine mistake has been made and can be substantiated, it may be beneficial to negotiate the way forward rather than forcing a builder to lose money. In this instance, you may benefit from employing a professional surveyor to oversee the negotiations.

## COST-SAVING EXERCISES

When you have received the quotes from the potential builders/contractors, you can start comparing them against each other. Do not be surprised if they have not broken down the costs in the same manner, as builders' and contractors' quotes will vary in respect of where they decide to *load* their profits and overheads.

### Discuss the quote

If you favour one builder/contractor over another but his quote is higher, it is worth inviting him to discuss the quote and to show him the other quotes that you have received.

It may well be that he is more expensive because his standards are higher or that he employs a foreman to oversee each project. You should find, however, that he will be happy to discuss the quote, and will more than likely trim the quote down closer to the alternative quotes that you have, or maybe match them.

It is at this point that you can start to go into detail about the specification and make the necessary changes to trim the quote down even more if required, by reducing the specification or by making other cost savings as set out in the examples below.

Some may stand by their quote and not be prepared to lower it, even if it means losing the job. This would suggest that they have estimated the job properly and that they have a good order book, which can also indicate a good reputation.

### Quotes under your budget
You may well be surprised to find that the quotes have come in lower than your anticipated budget. Do not be tempted to make rash decisions at this point, as you should always have a contingency sum to cover any unforeseen problems that may occur.

It is worth trying to get the builder/contractor to trim the quote down in any case, as even a small saving may pay for an additional luxury item. However, don't be too pushy if you don't have to be!

### Quotes over your budget

If, on the other hand, your budget costs are exceeded by, say, 15 per cent, do not be alarmed as there are many ways to make cost savings without compromising the quality of workmanship or materials. Builders will mainly use subcontractors for the specialist work and as such, they may have a high-mark up on certain elements of the work such as ceramic tiling and laminated floor finishes.

After you have eliminated these from the contract, you may be able to get alternative quotes at a later date from local contractors/suppliers. These may be as much as 30 per cent lower than that quoted in the builder's estimate.

The only downside of removing elements from the builder's package is that work on them then has to be coordinated with the builder's work. This can cause problems. Alternatively, you can have this work carried out at the end of the project once the main work is complete.

This obviously means that you will be inconvenienced for a longer period, although these sorts of specialist work are completed fairly quickly and there is less likelihood of damage being caused by other trades.

## Examples of cost savings

Areas in which cost savings may be made include:

◆ carrying out your own decoration;

◆ supplying your own sanitary ware;

◆ supplying your own carpets and soft furnishings;

◆ reducing the extent of external work to ensure the main works are complete;

◆ removing elements of work such as cornices, dado rails, ceramic tiling, mirrors, etc;

◆ reducing the specification, e.g. smaller skirting, less expensive ironmongery and fittings, less expensive light fittings, etc.

As you can see, there are many ways in which to make cost savings – you just need to examine your specification and prioritise accordingly.

## Organising your own plant, materials and labour

There is a further method to save costs: you organise all of the plant, material and labour yourself. This can result in savings of approximately 15–20 per cent.

However, if you are not experienced in this type of organising and negotiating on materials, etc., the savings could be very minimal. At the same time, it can be very time-consuming to say the least.

This will require some serious decision-making and research if you are to proceed with this method, as stress levels can go through the roof when things go wrong. It is therefore not advisable for first timers.

## TIMESCALE PROGRAMME OF WORKS

When inviting contractors to quote, it is important to ensure that a programme of works is included in the quote. This will show how long the builder/contractor anticipates working on your project.

When making comparisons, you should take into account the amount of time that you will be inconvenienced against the differences in the quotes. For example, one contractor may quote £35,000 for a two-storey extension that he estimates will take seven weeks, while another may quote £33,000 but estimate a timescale of ten weeks.

These are important issues, and they need serious consideration and discussion. Relations between client and contractor can quickly deteriorate when projects are not completed on or near the agreed timescale.

### Issuing your own timescale

On the other hand, you could issue your own preferred timescale with the tender documents. A rule of thumb here would be to use a figure of between £3,000 and £4,000 per week as the amount of labour and material to be spent on the project. Thus if your budget is £20,000 and you decide to use the figure of £4,000, you could suggest a time-frame of five weeks.

This method is for guidance only and applies to normal domestic work such as extensions and loft conversions. However, the nature of the work and the specification will also have a bearing on the duration of any project, and when there are technically difficult operations such as underpinning, timescales become nothing more than guestimates rather than true estimates.

Once the timescale is agreed, you need to ensure that a detailed timescale programme of works is issued with the quote. This will give you the opportunity to discuss any lack of progress as the project proceeds and the reasons for any delay.

### Unforeseen problems

It is worth pointing out at this stage that, while a builder or contractor may give you a timescale programme that he feels is achievable, the nature of building work is such that many unforeseen problems can occur. On small projects this can affect the programme to such a degree that it is very difficult to claw the time back.

Problems on the ground are usually costly, both in terms of money and time. This is where you need to be fully informed of what the problems are and what the likely additional costs and time will be, if any.

**Example of a programme of works**

Table 5.1 shows an example of a programme of works for a two-storey extension.

As you can see from this example, it is possible to see at a glance the specific dates at which each element occurs in relation to the progress of the project as a whole. By using a split pattern within the cells it is also possible to identify the specific days which must be adhered to for certain elements of work to be carried out, such as when service providers are expected to lay on their particular supplies, i.e. water, gas, etc.

## EXTRAS AND VARIATIONS

This is a very important area for discussion and is one that can cause a problem between the client and the contractor if the specification is not comprehensive.

It is an unfortunate fact that some builders/contractors are happy to quote for building works on specifications or descriptions of work that are very basic. If the builder supplies a written quote on poor information, there will not be sufficient details to separate so called 'extras' from what you believed to be part of the original specification.

Builders/contractors will know what is involved in the work that they are being asked to quote for, and some will make huge profits on work that clearly has to be carried out but which they subsequently invoice as an extra. Due to poor information and a client's lack of knowledge, some builders can be very convincing in these situations.

### Agree basis for charging and authorisation

It is inevitable that some extras or variations to the project will arise that need to be carried out. What you must discuss and agree on is whether this work will be carried out on an hourly or fixed priced basis. You must also endeavour to avoid extras or variations being carried out without your authorisation.

Any extras or variations must also be discussed only with the person with whom you placed the contract and not with anyone working for him, although this can sometimes be unavoidable. Write down all extras

**Name of project: 174 York Road**

| Description | Year | | | | | | | | | | |
|---|---|---|---|---|---|---|---|---|---|---|---|
| | **200X** | | | | | | | | | | |
| **Month** | **January** | | | | **February** | | | | **March** | | |
| **W/C** | 5 | 12 | 19 | 26 | 2 | 9 | 16 | 23 | 1 | 8 | 15 |
| 1. Site set-up and preparation, inc. drainage | ■ | | | | | | | | | | |
| 2. Excavation of foundation and concreting | | ■ | | | | | | | | | |
| 3. Build brickwork to DPC | | | | | | | | | | | |
| 4. Concrete oversite | | | | | | | | | | | |
| 5. Build blockwork and brickwork to first lift | | | ■ | | | | | | | | |
| 6. Scaffold first lift | | | | ■ | | | | | | | |
| 7. Build blockwork and brickwork to second lift | | | | ■ | | | | | | | |
| 8. Install floor joists and lay temp. floor | | | | | | | | | | | |
| 9. Scaffold second lift | | | | | ■ | | | | | | |
| 10. Build blockwork and brickwork to top lift | | | | | ■ | | | | | | |
| 11. Scaffold top lift | | | | | | | | | | | |
| 12. Install roof trusses and tie to existing roof | | | | | | ■ | | | | | |

| Task | | | | | | | | | | | | | | |
|---|---|---|---|---|---|---|---|---|---|---|---|---|---|---|
| 13. Fit new roofing felt, battens and tiles | ■ | | | | | | | | | | | | | |
| 14. First fix M and E | | ■ | ■ | | | | | | | | | | | |
| 15. First fix carpentry, including plasterboarding | | | ■ | ■ | | | | | | | | | | |
| 16. Install new windows and doors, inc. protection | | | | ■ | | | | | | | | | | |
| 17. Plastering and screeding | | | | | ■ | | | | | | | | | |
| 18. Second fix carpentry | | | | | | ■ | | | | | | | | |
| 19. Second fix M and E, including rainwater goods | | | | | | ■ | | | | | | | | |
| 20. Decoration internal and external | | | | | | | ■ | | | | | | | |
| 21. Reinstate external areas, new paving, etc. | | | | | | ■ | | | | | | | | |
| 22. Clear site | | | | | | | | | | | | | | |
| **Client's cost-saving elements** | | | | | | | | | | | | | | |
| 23. Fitted wardrobes | | | | | | | | | ■ | ■ | | | | |
| 24. Carpets | | | | | | | | | | | ■ | | | |
| 25. Ceramic tiling | | | | | | | | | | ■ | ■ | | | |
| 26. Specialist wall/floor finishes | | | | | | | | | | | | ■ | | |

Table 5.1 Sample timescale programme of works

or variations and remember that some of these variations could possibly involve cost savings.

### Obtaining a quote

If you do make changes to the scope of works or
specification, ensure that you obtain a quotation or
estimate for the new works before agreeing for the
work to proceed. Remember, once the builder/con-
tractor has been awarded the main contract, his prices
may not be as keen as when there is competition for
the work.

Bear in mind, though, that if a contractor has to bring
in outside assistance in addition to that which has been
planned, he may have to pay above the normal going
rate. However, this may sometimes be worth the
additional cost if it means that the project is completed
on schedule.

This could be an area open to discussion when
deciding on which builder/contractor to use. You could
have a mutual agreement that any additional work will
be at an agreed rate, or on a pro-rata basis of a certain
element which can be clearly identified.

Remember, however, *the more comprehensive your
specification is, the less likely it will be that your budget
will be overstretched.*

I cannot emphasise enough how important it is to ensure that the builder/contractor knows that you are not prepared to pay for additional work that has not been discussed.

One of the dangers of not having agreed procedures is that additional work can be claimed for which may not have actually been carried out! For example, I have heard of builders who have made huge sums of money from clients by *claiming* for hours of additional work for excavating for deeper foundations, a task which incurs heavy costs for the use of machinery, the removal of soil and the application of additional concrete. Clients who are not in control of their projects are susceptible to these types of scams.

## 6

# Starting the Work

### CONTRACT OF AGREEMENT

One of the most important documents that should be discussed with any builder or contractor is the contract of agreement. Whether it is a formal contract or one which has been mutually agreed upon, it may become a vital document in the event of any financial or contractual discrepancies.

Some contractors may ask you to enter into a contract with them, which would generally indicate a professional set-up. However, the domestic sector does not usually work with such safeguards.

The advantage of entering into a contract – especially when large sums of money are involved – is that you have a legal document which relates to the written quote from the contractor.

### What the contract should cover

The contract should include the terms of payment and any bonus/incentive clause as discussed in Chapter 7.

However, as clearly spelled out, these types of arrangement can only work when there are no changes to the specification, and when there are sufficient information and drawings to minimise any additional work or changes.

Included in this guidebook is a sample contract of agreement, which will give you an idea of what you need to cover. Alternatively, there are 'off-the-shelf' contracts available such as the JCT (Joint Contracts Tribunal) Building Contract for a home owner/occupier, as detailed below.

**Financial agreements**

Always have any financial agreement confirmed in writing, no matter how small the amount. It is the first thing that any legal representative will ask you for in the case of any form of dispute.

**Formal contracts**

A formal contract of agreement is meant to protect the interests of both parties, so if the contractor refuses to enter into such an agreement it may be best to choose one who does.

Formal contracts do not have to be sanctioned by a solicitor, but it is advisable to have a third party witness the agreement.

## 'Off-the-shelf' contracts

Alternatively, 'off-the-shelf' contracts are available such as the JCT (Joint Contracts Tribunal) Building Contract for a home owner/occupier which covers the areas outlined in Table 6.1.

---

**Part 1: The Arrangements for the Work**

A   The work to be done
B   Planning permission, building regulations and party walls
C   Using facilities on the premises
D   Price
E   Payment
F   The working period
G   Product guarantees
H   Insurances
I   Working hours
J   Occupation and security of the premises
K   Disputes

**Part 2: The Conditions**

1. Carrying out the work – contractor's responsibilities
2. Carrying out the work – customer's responsibilities
3. Health and safety
4. Changing the work details
5. Extending the work period
6. Payment
7. Contractor's continuing responsibility for faults in the work
8. Bringing the contract to an end, by either party
9. Insolvency
10. Other rights and remedies
11. Law of contract

---

Table 6.1 Coverage of the JCT Building Contract

The type of contract shown in Table 6.1 would normally be used in a situation which involves larger amounts of money but it is down to the discretion of the individual whether or not this contract is used.

In any case it is worthwhile obtaining a copy of the JCT contract so that you understand the responsibilities placed upon both the builder/contractor and yourself.

### Writing your own contract

You may decide to write your own contract but I do advise you to seek legal advice if you are in any doubt.

## METHOD STATEMENT

### What is a method statement?

This is not a document that the general public will necessarily be familiar with, and in fact most domestic builders will not have been required to produce one.

A method statement is a descriptive account of the way in which a particular operation will be carried out, for example what precautions the builder will be taking to ensure the security of your property, and how he will ensure the safety of all the people involved in the project.

### Requesting a method statement

It is not unreasonable for you to request a method statement, for example, for any work that may cause a

**Issued to:** Mr & Mrs Dogood

**Name of contractor:** J. Bloggs

**Circulation:**

Client        Architect

Surveyor     Other

**Date:** 25/12/02        **Job no.:** 111        **M.S. no.:** 1

**Site address:** The Red House, Redbridge Road

**Details of work:**
1: Remove existing window and replace with new UPVC window
2: Paint existing external wall and fix signage over door
3: Install 6 light bollards to illuminate pathway

**Location of work:**
1: Front of main building on Redbridge Road, above main entrance door
2: Front elevation to property, on Redbridge Road
3: Either side of footpath, as per drawing

**Plant to be used:**
1: Lightweight tower; 110 V Kango; angle grinder; percussion drill; cement mixer; jet washer

**Method to be adopted:**

**1:** Erect tower in accordance with instructions. Lay protection to tower and window to avoid glass falling. Remove glass and frame, bagging up all debris and taking to skip via main stairs. Take new window up to position via internal stairs.

**2:** Lay protection to ground, clean existing walls with jet wash system, and paint walls with exterior paint from lightweight tower.

**3:** Gun out holes in existing pathway for new light bollards, excavate trench in which armoured cables will be laid, install cables and bollards in accordance with maker's recommendations and relevant electrical regulations.

**Safety precautions to be taken:**

Place signage around work area to inform persons of men working above. Place physical barrier to force pedestrians to walk around work area.

First-aid box in workvan adjacent with one first aider on site.

In liaison with property owner, arrange alternative access and egress when main entrance door is obstructed by lightweight tower.

Ensure that all users of the property are fully informed of the activities, and timing of each element, by use of short-term bar chart posted on noticeboard

**Prepared by:**

Table 6.2 Sample method statement

security risk or safety issue, or where the sequence of work is important to minimise inconvenience.

A contractor may put up resistance to providing method statements. However, he only needs to discuss these elements with you, although the discussion should be recorded.

You may also be required to produce the information for your insurance company.

### Example of a method statement

Table 6.2 provides an example of the type of information that would be covered in a method statement: details of the work or works, the location of the work or works, the plant to be used, the method to be adopted for each element of the works, and where and how precautions will be taken.

### Other documentation

Further information associated with the method statement may also be issued, such as a short-term bar chart showing, for example, how long certain areas will be out of action (see Table 6.3). This shows how such documents can assist in the smooth running of the work, as they enable you to make allowances and change any arrangements that may be affected by it.

Such short-term bar charts are easy to prepare and do not need to be produced by computer. However, they are much more practical when they are computer-generated as the formatted documents can be used in several useful ways.

## INSPECTION PROCEDURE

It is very important to establish a procedure for inspecting all works on a regular basis. Ensure that you inform the contractor in writing of anything that is giving you cause for concern. For example, short-term bar charts can be used to highlight areas of high activity and when there will be factors which affect incoming services such as electricity and gas. These charts can also be used to update the main timescale programme. By leaving spare lines, any additional or extra work can also be inserted.

It would not be unreasonable to ask the builder/contractor to accompany you on these inspections as it is much easier to explain your dissatisfaction with or indeed your approval of the work as it proceeds. This will also give the builder/contractor the opportunity to give explanations. For example, it may be that the work is not ready to be offered as complete.

It is always advisable to inspect the works as items progress or as they are completed. Not only will this

**Project:** Example

| | Month | | | | | | | | | | | | | | | | | | | | |
|---|---|---|---|---|---|---|---|---|---|---|---|---|---|---|---|---|---|---|---|---|---|
| | **Day** | M | T | W | T | F | S | S | M | T | W | T | F | S | S | M | T | W | T | F |
| | **Date** | | | | | | | | | | | | | | | | | | | | |
| **RENEW WINDOW** | | | | | | | | | | | | | | | | | | | | | |
| 1. Place barriers in position | | | | | | | | | | | | | | | | | | | | | |
| 2. Remove existing window | | | | | | | | | | | | | | | | | | | | | |
| 3. Install new window | | | | | | | | | | | | | | | | | | | | | |
| 4. Make good inside reveals | | | | | | | | | | | | | | | | | | | | | |
| 5. Fix new window board | | | | | | | | | | | | | | | | | | | | | |
| 6. Decorate internal walls | | | | | | | | | | | | | | | | | | | | | |
| 7. Main doorway out of action | | | | | | | | | | | | | | | | | | | | | |
| **PAINT EXISTING WALL** | | | | | | | | | | | | | | | | | | | | | |
| 1. Lay protection | | | | | | | | | | | | | | | | | | | | | |
| 2. Erect lightweight towers | | | | | | | | | | | | | | | | | | | | | |
| 3. Jet wash wall | | | | | | | | | | | | | | | | | | | | | |
| 4. Apply sealer to wall | | | | | | | | | | | | | | | | | | | | | |

5. Apply first coat to wall

6. Apply second coat to wall

7. Apply top coat to wall

8. Clean windows and inspect work

9. Remove towers and protection

10. Make good any disturbance

11. Main doorway out of action

**FIT NEW LIGHTING BOLLARDS**

1. Set up physical barriers

2. Excavate for lights and cables

3. Install cables and bollards, concrete

4. Connect cables to bollards

5. Make connection to fuse board

6. Test and commission lights

7. Make good any disturbance

8. Remove physical barriers

Table 6.3 Sample short-term programme bar chart

give the contractor the impression that you are taking an active interest in the quality of the work, but it will also provide an opportunity to discuss and correct items before it is too late.

### Problems with subcontractors

Builders and contractors rely on subcontractors and sometimes have difficulty in getting them on site when required, particularly in boom times. Let the main contractor's staff know if there is a problem before they leave the site, as it may be difficult to get the subcontractor back to rectify any defects once they have started another contract elsewhere.

Always put your concerns in writing and remember to inform the main contractor as the first point of contact.

Although we have stated that a contract of agreement should be in place together with any financial agreement, if there are ever serious concerns or disputes, it is always advisable to try and sort out any problems amicably before having to implement any contractual/legal obligations.

### SITE SET-UP

This is an area that needs some discussion before the builder/contractor starts on your project, as facilities such as a canteen, toilet and office may be on site from start to finish. Some site facilities may need to be dropped into position by crane, depending on the size of the project.

There is a number of issues relevant to your project that you may need to clarify. It is worth making a list of those that you can think of. A sample site consideration checklist of some of the many issues that can form part of one single project is included in Table 6.4.

| Description | | Action |
|---|---|---|
| Parking restrictions | Y | No parking on verge |
| Storing of material | Y | On client's driveway |
| Skip position | Y | On road |
| Portable toilet | Y | On client's driveway |
| Scaffolding | Y | Back extension |
| Security | Y | Alarmed scaffold |
| Water facilities | Y | By client's outside tap |
| Power facilities | N | Generator |
| Client's considerations | Y | Beware of plants |
| Noise restrictions | Y | 8.00 a.m.–6.00 p.m. working hours |
| Delivery times | N | Normal |
| Photos | Y | Damaged footpath prior to start |
| Local authority | Y | Builder to inform for inspections, etc. |
| Crane required | N | |
| Facilities available | | WC, drinking water |
| Warning of very dusty work | | Effect on cars, etc. |
| Responsibility for arranging services | | Electricity, water, gas, etc. |

Table 6.4 Sample site consideration checklist

As you can see from Table 6.4, there are issues that need to be discussed prior to the project starting as they have the potential to create difficulties between the client and the builder/contractor.

### Getting through the red tape

There are some elements that the builder/contractor may be better equipped to deal with. For example, they may have connections within some organisations/ service providers who can speed up some of the red tape that can slow the project down.

Most of these types of issue will require you to make extra payments that would not normally be included in the contractor's quote, such as payment for crossovers from the road or the cost of increasing the size of electricity intake cables or water feeds if required.

While most incoming domestic service supplies will normally be adequate to take the extra loading, it is worth keeping in mind that additional costs may occur if heavier loading is necessary.

### Site instruction for additional work

When you do have to instruct the builder/contractor to carry out additional work, it is worth using a pre-formatted sheet such as the site instruction form illustrated in Table 9.1. This includes particular information such as dates, a description of the work and sketches where possible. This will help to avoid misunderstandings and can include approximate costs and timing.

# 7

# Financial Arrangements

## VALUATION OF WORK COMPLETED

If you are financing the project yourself, it is advisable not to pay money up front if you can help it. You need to make any potential builder/contractor aware of your estimated budget and that you will be making stage payments (see below).

When there is plenty of building work available, or if a builder/contractor has had a bad experience whereby he did not receive full payment from a previous client, he may ask for money up front. However, it is not advisable to pay any money in advance as you will not have any control over the project if you do.

If a contractor comes recommended to you and fulfils all of the criteria for being able to carry out the work but is asking for money up front, you would be advised to explain that, due to constraints on your financial arrangements for financing the work, you can only pay for work carried out.

We mentioned in Chapter 6 that terms of payment should be agreed in the contract, or at the very least confirmed in writing.

### Valuations for stage payments

A mortgage company may finance a project on the condition that payments are made on completion of certain stages, and may have a surveyor/inspector visit the property to ascertain the value of work carried out.

These stages are the basis on which the valuations are made and include the amount of labour and material that has been put into the project. You need to be certain that the contractor understands these requirements and is prepared to finance the project up to these stages.

## CONTINGENCY PLANS

It is advisable to have a contingency plan in place to cover any unforeseen financial circumstances, as highlighted in Chapter 2. The construction industry is one which can sometimes throw up a problem that requires a complete reassessment of a project.

One example of this often occurs with the foundations of buildings. Engineers design the foundations in relation to the weight that the building will produce and the ground conditions locally. Unfortunately ground conditions do not always prove to be what was expected, and when foundations need to be considerably deeper than anticipated, this can involve more excavating or piling.

This in turn leads to more spoil being removed and more concrete put in its place.

In more extreme cases, thousands of pounds extra may have to be found to cover the cost. Strict monitoring of these elements will help to avoid the uncertainty of additional costs.

There are many other unforeseen circumstances that can occur as discussed in previous chapters. For this reason you are advised to hold back some of your original budget.

If you find that you are out of the ground and have been fortunate not to have incurred extra costs, the likelihood of further unforeseen circumstances arising is slim. You can then think about upgrading your specification or having extra work carried out.

## MAKING PAYMENTS

Once the valuation has been agreed based on the amount of work that has been carried out and assuming standards are satisfactory, payment can be made.

It is advisable to have an agreement to pay within seven days of the valuation so that the contractor will have carried out a further week's work rather than be paid up to date. This is merely a safeguard, and will be in keeping with business transactions generally. *Always* get a signed receipt for any money that is paid out.

### The final payment

Once the building works are complete and you are satisfied that your standards have been achieved, you need to ensure that you have all test certificates and warranties in place before you make the final payment.

Items such as central heating components and new boilers will have warranties and guarantees, and will require certification before they are handed over as complete. This also applies to new electrical installations, and full tests and test results need to be produced for possible inspection by the building control officer.

When building regulation applications are made, the client can request a 'completion certificate' from the building inspector to certify that the main works are completed to his specification.

Lending institutions often require this. If this is the case, you need to ensure that the builder/contractor provides these certificates in order for the money to be released to him.

## BONUS/INCENTIVE SCHEMES

Such schemes could be put in place where a client stands to lose out financially if the project overruns. With mutual agreement you could introduce an incentive bonus arrangement based on the project being completed on or within the agreed time.

The bonus would be worked out on the number of weeks or days under the agreed period. You need to be mindful of two things if you enter into such a scheme: any additional work can affect the finishing date, and your specification needs to be very comprehensive.

The likelihood of the project being complete way ahead of schedule is slim, whereas projects overrunning are common. If you do enter into such an agreement and you find that the project has overrun the programmed dates, there may be justifiable reasons for this which would have been covered in the site meetings.

Bonus/incentive schemes are used in large commercial projects in conjunction with penalty clauses if the project does overrun. The amount of bonus or penalties is worked out on a percentage of costs that the client stands to gain or lose through early or late completion of the project.

These schemes are rarely used in the domestic side of the industry, and should only be considered where both parties fully understand the consequences. It is advisable to contact your legal representative before drawing up such an agreement.

## 8

# Operation and Maintenance Manuals

## OPERATION MANUALS

With all new installations, whether they are mechanical, electrical or other, such as windows, doors, etc., there are always operating instructions. You must ensure that the contractor hands these over to you and where necessary arranges a demonstration.

If you do not receive sufficient training in the operation of the installed equipment and as a result manage to break something through the application of force or by following the wrong procedure, you may invalidate any guarantees that apply.

All new equipment does take a little time to understand how it operates, particularly now that many systems are controlled digitally. Do not be afraid to ask for the time necessary for you to understand how the equipment works – remember that people who install such equipment work with it on a regular basis and may become complacent about other people's lack of technical knowledge.

If you have arranged for the equipment to be supplied and have asked for it to be installed during the project, you may find that the electrical contractor for argument's sake may not be as willing to spend the time to give you a demonstration. In fact, if it is equipment that he is not familiar with, he may not understand how it operates himself.

Always ensure that, if you buy equipment from a shop, you fully understand how to operate it. Shops will normally be happy to spend the time required, particularly if it secures a sale!

## MAINTENANCE MANUALS

Again, maintenance manuals should accompany all new installations. It is vitally important that these are read and understood, as any guarantees may be affected if they are not complied with. Do ensure that if a certain piece of equipment requires periodic tests and inspections these are marked on your yearly calendar or in your personal diary.

Depending on the piece of equipment involved, there may be a requirement that it be maintained or tested by a particular company which is certified to carry out such work. This is something that needs special attention, as a person or company not certified by the manufacturers could invalidate the guarantee if maintenance is carried out wrongly, or if the maintenance manuals are not stamped with the appropriate certificated technician's stamp.

## TEST CERTIFICATES

During the course of the works there are certain elements that require tests to be carried out and certified. It is advisable to ask the contractor for copies of such tests to add to your documents. These tests are normally associated with mechanical and electrical work. However, there are other inspections that the builder/contractor is obliged to inform the building control officer about, which we referred to in Chapter 1.

## GUARANTEES

Many guarantees do not come into effect until such time as they are registered and this is one aspect that is regularly overlooked. You need to ensure that all manufacturers' guarantees are handed over to you at the end of the project and sent off to the appropriate departments.

It is worth considering extending the guarantee period or taking out additional cover for equipment, as it can be very costly to repair electrical or mechanical items. In fact, the cost of repair can sometimes be greater than buying a replacement.

Guarantees that should be handed over include:

- central heating equipment and plumbing fittings;
- electrical installation equipment and fittings;
- UPVC or aluminium windows and doors;
- appliances;
- specialist works, i.e. laminate flooring, kitchen unit fittings, etc.;
- damp-proof injection;
- waterproof rendering;
- specialist flat roof systems;
- Velux windows;
- door furniture;
- data cabling equipment;
- specialist external paint systems;
- telephone/aerial equipment.

**Monitoring maintenance/inspection periods**

In order to be able to monitor the inspection or maintenance periods of new installations at a glance, you could produce a sheet of the relevant information, have it laminated and attach it to a noticeboard or put it up somewhere where it will be on view. It is very easy to forget dates for inspections and maintenance periods, particularly if there are long gaps between them.

The fact that you could invalidate the guarantee by not adhering to them should give you the incentive to put into place a system to remind you of the specific dates.

As you can see from the example in Table 8.1, it is very easy to produce such a chart, even by hand. You can also include a column for the telephone numbers of the appropriate people to contact.

### General inspection procedures

In the column titled *Inspection period,* you will notice that some of the equipment has 'General' written in the cell. This is because you may not need to have a test or inspection that has to be recorded. It is advisable, however, to have a good look at certain areas period-ically that may not be on view in everyday use.

With elements such as damp-proof injection, for example, it is worth checking behind units and inspecting wallpaper for signs of dampness as these can mask continuing problems. This can also be said for water-proof rendering and specialist external paint systems.

While laminate floor systems are desirable in bath-rooms and kitchens, it is worth paying for good

| Equipment/ item | Guarantee period | Inspection period | Date installed | Next inspection |
|---|---|---|---|---|
| Central heating equipment | 3 years | Yearly | Jan. 200X | Jan. 200Y |
| Electrical control panel and equipment | 1 year | Yearly | Feb. 200X | Feb. 200Y |
| UPVC windows and doors | 2 years | General | Mar. 200X | Feb. 200Y |
| Laminate flooring | 1 year 6 months | General | Mar. 200X | Aug. 200Y |
| Damp-proof injection | 15 years | General | Jan. 200X | Jan. 200Y |
| Waterproof rendering | 10 years | General | Feb. 200X | Feb. 200Y |
| Specialist flat roof systems | 25 years | General | Mar. 200X | Mar. 200Y |
| Velux windows | 3 years | General | Feb. 200X | Feb. 200Y |
| Specialist external paint systems | 10 years | General | Mar. 200X | Mar. 200Y |
| Telephone/aerial equipment | 1 year | General | Jan. 200X | Jan. 200Y |
| Cooker | 3 years | General | Mar. 200X | Mar. 200Y |
| Fire alarm | 5 years | 6 monthly | Feb. 200X | Aug. 200Y |
| Washing machine | 3 years | General | Mar. 200X | Mar. 200Y |
| Burglar alarm | 3 years | 6 monthly | Mar. 200X | Sep. 200Y |

Table 8.1 Sample inspection/maintenance chart

quality. Pay good attention to the maintenance and cleaning procedures – many people do not use the correct cleaning agents and as a result find that water ingress causes problems that are not covered under the guarantee.

# 9

# Good Working Relations

## FIRST MEETING WITH MAIN CONTRACTOR

Before the start of the project, you need to hold a meeting with the main contractor to establish a regular timeframe for site meetings and other pre-contract issues. This first meeting needs to be at your property and with a senior member of the main contractor's team or the contractor himself.

Your first meeting agenda should include:

◆ site set-up (site consideration checklist);
◆ visitors;
◆ site instructions;
◆ inspections/quality control;
◆ environmental issues;
◆ welfare facilities;
◆ health and safety issues;
◆ site meetings.

## SITE SET-UP

When the time comes to start the project, you should know where the builder/contractor plans to set up the site office and any welfare facilities (if applicable). You need to be satisfied that their plans are not going to cause you unnecessary inconvenience.

### Site consideration checklist

In order to make life easier, a site consideration checklist is useful to eliminate elements that are not required and those that will need to be prioritised, as discussed in Chapter 6.

The checklist should include:

- site office size and position;
- parking restrictions;
- storage of material (including protection);
- skip position;
- portable toilet (if applicable);
- scaffolding (security arrangements);
- water facilities;
- power facilities;
- noise restrictions (if applicable);
- delivery times (site working hours);
- photographs (pavement and road).

There may also be many other considerations, depending on the nature and location of the project. Some builders or companies will have a person who deals with site planning, analysing all aspects of the work from local traffic controls to where the site toilet will be situated. However, this level of planning is usually associated with the commercial side of the construction industry.

It is important to discuss these issues in detail, as they can cause client/contractor problems even if the standard of work is very high.

## VISITORS

If the work is to be carried out while you are not at the property during the day, you must ensure that the security and privacy of your home is not compromised by any unauthorised visitors. You must let the builder/contractor know that only visitors who have an active role to play in the project will be allowed access, and that employees of the builder/contractor are aware of these instructions.

In order to ensure that these risks are minimised, it would be advisable to issue the builder/contractor with a list of people who may need to have access to the property. These may include representatives of elements of the project that you are dealing with yourself, such as carpet suppliers, kitchen suppliers, specialist finishing contractors, etc.

It would be advisable, however, to arrange to meet any representatives of companies that you are dealing with yourself at a mutually agreed time to ensure that the correct information is passed on.

Some reps will assume that the builder/contractor knows all of the specific details of the project and may be given information that is acted upon, only to find later that the information was incorrect. In this situation, the project could be delayed because alterations to, or a complete reinstallation of equipment is required. This would definitely cause problems all round.

The site foreman should have a site diary in which all site visitors are recorded, and which you must be informed of at site meetings. If an inspection of some description has been carried out, information should be recorded in the diary against the name of the person who made the inspection together with any comments or results.

It is important to let the builder/contractor know that if his employees see anyone on site who should not be there, they should ask them to leave the site immediately.

## SITE INSTRUCTIONS

As mentioned in Chapter 5, it is inevitable that there will be some extras or variations. It is, therefore, very important to establish a method of controlling the cost and time factors relating to them.

Recording the information and issuing site instructions is one method of ensuring that you maintain control of additional work being carried out. It is, therefore, important that this issue is fully discussed and it is understood that the main contractor is not to carry out any additional work without a site instruction being issued (see Table 9.1), unless it is absolutely unavoidable.

Before any additional work is carried out, you need to be sure that your budget can be adjusted to accommodate the work and that you are fully aware of the implications with regard to the expected completion date.

The site instruction is a very useful and effective way of avoiding misunderstandings and disagreements on agreed works between you and the main contractor. Most subcontractors will have an identified role to play in the project. However, they will not usually carry out additional work unless instructed by the main contractor. It is advisable to always issue site instructions through the main contractor wherever possible.

If you find yourself in the situation where you need the subcontractor to carry out additional work and the main contractor is not available, the site instruction will usually allay any fears he may have of not getting

| SITE INSTRUCTION | | |
|---|---|---|
| **Issued to:**<br><br>**Name of contractor:** | **Circulation:**<br><br>**Client**<br><br>**Surveyor** | **Architect**<br><br>**Other** |
| **Date:** | | **SI no.:** |
| **Site address:** | | |
| **Details of work:**<br><br>**Location:** | | |
| **Materials used:**<br><br>**Labour content:** | | |
| All works carried out in this instruction are subject to a re-measure and will be taken into account in forthcoming valuations or final accounts. | | |
| **Sketches:** | | |
| **Name:** | | |

Table 9.1 Sample site instruction form

paid for the work. The site instruction will also form part of the documentation for the final account. These instructions may also show where savings have been made!

## INSPECTIONS/QUALITY CONTROL

It is important to carry out your own inspections and to agree to inspect the work at each site meeting with the main contractor. If there are any issues that you are not quite happy with, you must bring these to the attention of the main contractor at your earliest opportunity. However, you must bear in mind that until works are offered to you as complete, some work may look below standard when in fact it is in mid process. The main contractor should be able to explain these processes.

As far as quality control is concerned, it is the main contractor's responsibility to ensure that the material and labour meet the required standards. This includes all works carried out by subcontractors.

If in the unlikely event the main contractor tries to pass responsibility over to you for ensuring quality control of work that he is responsible for, you need to remind him that the reason for employing a builder/contractor in the first place was to ensure quality and standards are placed in the hands of professionals in this field.

## ENVIRONMENTAL ISSUES

There are laws governing the burning of waste material and the disposal of material such as asbestos, etc. It is very important to discuss the possibility that there may be hazardous waste on your project even if you are uncertain. You need to be satisfied that the main contractor knows his obligations in this matter and that he is to inform you of any such findings.

## WELFARE FACILITIES

The type of work that is to be carried out and your specific requirements with regard to the security of your property will dictate what kind of facilities will be provided for the contractors.

Under the Health and Safety at Work Act 1974 and the Management of Health and Safety at Work Act 1999, employers are required to provide rest facilities during work hours and eating facilities during rest breaks. Employers must also provide adequate sanitary conveniences with hot and cold running water.

On small domestic projects that do not have sufficient space for site cabins, etc. the client would normally come to an arrangement whereby the contractors would use the client's basic facilities, i.e. WC, water and electricity supplies. If, on the other hand, you do have space and the project involves many different trades, etc. it is advisable to insist on the main contractor making their own welfare facility arrangements.

This could mean that they require water and electrical supplies to a site cabin. However, there are facilities that can be hired by the main contractor which are completely self-contained and can be independently powered by a small generator.

## HEALTH AND SAFETY ISSUES

During the course of the project there will be progress meetings which will have a set agenda for the main issues. However, before the project starts you must discuss the potential risks with regard to anyone living at or visiting the property during the work.

Typical questions to ask include the following:

♦ Is there going to be a scaffold, and if so what measures will be put in place to stop unauthorised persons gaining access outside of normal working hours?

♦ What measures will be taken to avoid excessive dust and noise affecting you and your neighbours (particularly where there are cars close by)?

♦ How often will the debris be removed from site, and by what means?

♦ If there are to be any deep excavations, what measures will be taken to avoid anyone falling in?

◆ Can you see a copy of the main contractor's health and safety policy? Employers who employ more than five employees are required to produce a written statement of their policy on health and safety, and the organisation and arrangements that are in place to bring that policy into effect.

There will obviously be other questions which you may wish to ask, depending on the size and nature of the project.

## SITE MEETINGS

Once you have agreed on the frequency of site meetings, it is important to establish the issues that will be discussed and exactly what information you will expect to receive at these meetings. If the main contractor is not in the habit of producing reports to highlight progress, etc., it would not be unreasonable for you to issue an agenda and take notes of the verbal discussion.

These meetings and the recording of information discussed will undoubtedly be of vital importance during the course of the project, particularly when finalising payments for additional work. It is at these meetings that specifics are normally discussed in detail.

### The agenda

The agenda should include the following issues:

◆ progress against programme;
◆ health and safety issues;
◆ external issues (neighbours, etc.);
◆ delays;
◆ information required;
◆ additional work;
◆ any other business.

### Progress against programme

By looking at the progress against programme sheet (see Table 9.2) you can see at a glance the areas that have fallen behind and those that are ahead of schedule. Each area can be discussed in order as they appear on the programme. It would also be useful if you can agree that the main contractor provides you with a brief description of each element and how it affects the overall programme.

### Health and safety issues

Health and safety issues need to be included even if the main contractor has nothing to report, as there may be issues that *you* would like to discuss. You may need to know any site activities that will require warning the neighbours that there will be excessive noise or dust.

| Element | Brief overview | Progress % | Actual % |
|---|---|---|---|
| Enabling works | On schedule | 100 | 100 |
| Demolition | Delayed due to weather | 100 | 80 |
| Set out new work | On schedule | 60 | 60 |
| Alter drainage | On schedule | 40 | 40 |
| Dig footings | Delayed due to weather | 20 | 10 |
| Brickwork to 1st floor | | | |
| 1st floor joists | | | |
| Brickwork to plate | | | |
| Install new steels | | | |
| Roof covering | | | |
| Windows and doors | | | |
| Fascia and soffit | | | |
| Fire escape stairs | | | |
| Work to stairs | | | |
| 1st fix carpentry | | | |
| Plastering | | | |
| 2nd fix carpentry | | | |
| 2nd fix M & E | | | |
| Make good floors | | | |
| Decoration | | | |
| Clean and handover | | | |
| **Additional items** | | | |

Table 9.2 Sample progress against programme sheet

### External issues

External issues cover unforeseen circumstances beyond your control that may need your intervention or assistance, i.e. warning neighbours of activities that require full use of parking spaces, trimming back of neighbours' trees, etc.

### Delays

Delays need to be discussed at each meeting and whether or not the time can be pulled back. Clients who are warned of possible delays in advance tend to be more understanding, particularly if they are made fully aware of the reasons.

### Information required

Information required would normally be requested by the main contractor during the course of the project, but it is a sign of good management if you can pre-empt any answers to questions that they may need, well in advance of them actually asking.

### Additional work

As it is likely that there will be additional work, you must discuss the financial implications of this at the earliest opportunity. Additional work can include many small elements of work which can amount to much more than you realise when added together.

### Any other business

This is usually on the agenda to give the members of the meeting the opportunity to discuss any issues that have not otherwise been covered. During the course of the meeting, it is inevitable that decisions would have been made on financial and contractual matters. These matters and anything that has a bearing on the project that has been discussed, should be confirmed with the main contractor at the earliest opportunity. This will give him a chance to contact you if there are any misunderstandings before proceeding too far with his interpretation of what was said.

## CORRESPONDENCE

You will have learnt from this guidebook that written evidence of quotes, specifications, contracts and so on is very important. Any professional contractor will be only too happy to receive and send written confirmation of any contractual correspondence, which could include confirmation of verbal agreements and requests for information. If you enter into any form of contract with only verbal agreements, you are leaving yourself wide open in the event of anything going wrong.

## AVOIDING CONFLICT

The construction industry, by its very nature, is one that can cause inconvenience to the client, neighbours, local businesses and the general public. It can be very frustrating to have to endure dust and noise for weeks on end. It is therefore advisable to inform your neighbours and others who may be affected by the work. This will enable them to make allowances.

Your contractor should furnish you with enough information about how he intends running the project for there not to be any nasty surprises. In any eventuality it is important to maintain good working relations and confirm any concerns that you may have in writing rather than getting into conflict.

If the builder's or the contractor's employees or any of the subcontractors are not behaving in a responsible manner or are not adhering to agreements that have been made with regard to security measures, for example, you need to bring this to the attention of the senior person on site.

If the situation does not improve, then you must inform the builder/contractor both verbally and in writing, and if necessary ask for the offending person to be removed from your project.

## SITE TIDINESS

One of the first things that is noticed by all visitors to a project is how messy or tidy a site is. It is a fact that people form opinions of companies and individuals by first appearances. The main contractor may be able to turn out a good standard of work but if he does it in a messy environment, it counts for nothing.

It is not unreasonable for you to emphasise that the project needs to be as tidy as possible at all times. This would highlight the main contractor's professionalism and would ensure that you and any visitors that you may have during the course of the project are not exposed to any dangers.

No site will ever be 100 per cent tidy or 100 per cent safe but it is important to 'minimise the risk'. You need to ensure that standards are maintained and that the main contractor has the correct signs and security procedures in place. This is much easier to monitor if the site is tidy.

If the builder/contractor knows that you will be expecting high standards generally, the chances are you will get them.

## PHOTOGRAPHIC RECORDS

It is advisable to take plenty of photographs of the work as it proceeds. Apart from the opportunity to look back and see how your property has changed, it would be crucial evidence should things go wrong.

Some contractors feel uncomfortable when clients take photos, but this is easily remedied by telling them that you are taking them to show your friends the changes – and that they may be used for his portfolio once the project is satisfactorily completed.

If you have any reservations about any aspect of the work either before or during the contract, you must inform the main contractor straightaway.

# 10

# Record-keeping

## ISSUING DRAWINGS

From the very outset of any building or home improvement project, no matter how small, you should have produced sketches or scaled drawings. Whether you have produced your own drawings or have had them drawn up by a professional, it is very important to keep a simple drawing register (see Table 10.1).

Whenever you issue any sketches or drawings, they should be dated and given a number. Remember that you should always try to issue copies of the original rather than give your own copy away.

### Recording changes

If any changes are made to the drawings, the previous drawings should be marked as superseded, and the new drawing should be dated and given a revision code which would normally start with A. Any further revisions would continue with alphabetical revision codes. When a drawing or sketch is reissued, apart

**Sample drawing register**

| Title | 1 | 2 | 3 | 4 | 5 | 6 | 7 | 8 |
|---|---|---|---|---|---|---|---|---|
| Drawing no. | LS 01 | LS 02 | LS 03 | LS 04 | GC 225 | LS 05 | SK 556 | PD 324 |
| Date | 11/8/03 | 11/8/03 | 23/8/03 | 23/8/03 | 26/9/03 | 30/9/03 | 11/11/03 | 3/12/03 |
| Revision | A | | ~~A~~ B | | A | ~~A B~~ C | | ~~A B C~~ D |
| 1. Plan ground floor | 1/10/03 | | | | | | | |
| 2. Plan first floor | | 6/10/03 | | | | | | |
| 3. Roof plan | | | 6/10/03 | | | | | |
| 4. Elevations | | | | 6/10/03 | | | | |
| 5. Engineer's drawings | | | | | 16/10/03 | | | |
| 6. Drainage | | | | | | 6/10/03 | | |
| 7. Kitchen layout | | | | | | | 9/11/03 | |
| 8. Mechanical and electrical | | | | | | | | 9/12/03 |

Table 10.1 Sample drawing register

from the revision code, you should also make a note of the date that you received it.

As you can see from this simple example in Table 10.1, drawings are numbered and dated and they will also show any revisions that have been made. The information on most drawings relating to numbers, dates and revisions are usually found in the bottom right-hand corner. Always revise the dates on your register to the date of the revision or the date that you received or issued it.

Some architects will issue a drawing register which should have the appropriate boxes for updating changes, etc. These drawing registers are usually more detailed than the example shown in Table 10.1 but are very easy to understand once you have studied them.

You must always ensure that the builder/contractor is working to the current drawings. Late changes or outdated information will add to the project cost and may extend the programme, and if the responsibility for supplying information is yours the builder/contractor may be entitled to claim an extension to the time if the information is late.

Where the specification needs to be changed to suit unforeseen circumstances, it is important to identify who is responsible for detailing the changes. It may be that the architect will need to make some changes to the drawing, or the engineer may need to make alterations to the structural calculations, for example.

If this occurs it is important that the information required has been requested and confirmed in writing, to ensure that the continuity of work is not interrupted to an unacceptable degree.

## PROJECT FILE

In order to keep a track of all correspondence and information relating to the project, it is worth starting a project file with separate sections for the different elements involved. It would not be unusual to have 14 sections or more, so that you can easily access the information, for example:

- architect;
- engineer;
- contract drawings;
- programmes;
- specification;
- building contractor;
- local authority;
- contract documents;
- utilities companies;
- operation and maintenance manuals;

◆ insurance details;

◆ payment details;

◆ specialist contractors;

◆ miscellaneous (it is worth starting additional sections with new headings, although anything can end up in this section and be difficult to find).

## DIARY

It is very important to keep a diary of all telephone calls and a brief description of what was discussed, any action that you have been asked to carry out, and confirmation of any agreements that have been made.

If you change the specification for any reason, make sure that you inform the builder/contractor in writing the details of those changes. Any changes that are made may have financial implications, and you will need to know either way what these costs are. Contractors do not particularly like to reduce the cost of the work even if the amount of work has been reduced.

If possible you should also record an account of the work carried out each day, the labour on site each day and any problems that may have occurred. It would be advisable to inform the builder/contractor that you are keeping a progress diary and if for any justifiable reason he will not be on site on a particular day, that you would like to be informed so that you can make allowances if the project starts to overrun.

Builders and contractors who keep the client informed of progress – or lack of it – will help to avoid any frustration building up through lack of information or understanding.

It is also advisable to keep a record of the weather as this may affect the completion date.

## TELEPHONE NUMBERS

During the course of any project you will inevitably gather many telephone numbers related to the project. These can be entered in a single page in your diary under five headings:

◆ professional team: architect, engineer, BCO;
◆ building contractor and allied trades;
◆ services: gas, electric, telephone, water, etc.;
◆ emergency numbers generally;
◆ suppliers.

It is important that the builder issues you with the telephone numbers of his contractors in the event that you are unable to contact him (see Table 10.2), subject to the type of work being carried out. These would normally include:

- scaffolding company;
- roofer;
- electrician;
- plumber;
- glazier.

| Operation | Company | Name | Telephone | Fax | Mobile |
|---|---|---|---|---|---|
| Builder | | | | | |
| Roofer | | | | | |
| Scaffolding company | | | | | |
| Electrician | | | | | |
| Plumber | | | | | |
| Glazier | | | | | |
| Building control | | | | | |
| Architect | | | | | |
| Engineer | | | | | |
| Gas supplier | | | | | |
| Electric supplier | | | | | |
| Water supplier | | | | | |
| Telephone company | | | | | |
| Skip supplier | | | | | |

Table 10.2 Sample diary sheet for telephone numbers

As you can see from the example in Table 10.2, by keeping at hand a record of the telephone numbers of all the key people involved in the project, you will not have to leaf through a lot of files, which can be very frustrating when a number is required in a hurry.

# 11

# Professional and Site Teams

## THE CONSTRUCTION TEAM

Construction companies are usually categorised as large, medium or small. It is the small companies which usually carry out domestic work, which as a rule of thumb for a two-storey extension to a three-bedroom terraced house could be in the region of £25–£35,000, whereas an extension to a large 4–5 bedroom detached house could be in the region of £50–£100,000.

Obviously these figures can vary considerably depending on specification. However, this type of work would normally be carried out by companies categorised as small.

Since this guidebook is aimed mainly at the domestic market, I will not go into detail about the different roles of the professional departments within large and medium-sized companies. However, the organisation chart presented in Figure 11.1 will give you a picture of the typical management structure of a small company.

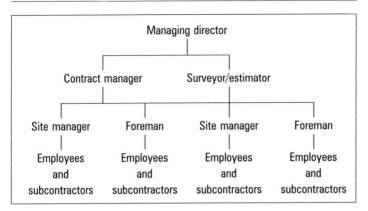

Figure 11.1 Typical management structure for a small construction company

## RESPONSIBILITIES OF SITE MANAGEMENT

### Site manager

Site managers do not usually carry out any practical work and are normally appointed to projects which require close coordination of subcontractors and precise continuity of material. These projects would normally be in the range of £400,000 and upwards. However, on projects that are technically difficult or have a very tight timescale, the range could start as low as £150,000.

It is the site manager's duty to ensure that the day-to-day running of the site is carried out to meet the regulations that are laid down by the construction industry regulatory bodies. He must ensure that site personnel are adequately trained and competent for the tasks which they are being asked to carry out.

Site managers are usually given the responsibility to make decisions which have a direct bearing on the site and the well-being of anyone affected by it. This would include the client, visitors (whether invited or not) and the immediate neighbours, among many others.

If the site manager is unable to satisfy your requirements for any reason, it is at this point that you should contact his superior. This could be the contract manager or director of the company.

If the project does not warrant a full time site manager, there must be an appointed person who is responsible for the site activities and health and safety requirements such as first aid, etc. Site managers who work on the domestic side of construction generally tend to come from a trade background and therefore have a very good understanding of all of the elements involved.

Site managers will not only take on the responsibility of coordinating the labour and material, they will also be responsible for requesting information from the professional teams. There are systems for managing sites which ensure that the flow of information once the project is underway does not significantly slow the project down.

Where there is a significant complication or delay which could not have been foreseen, this will be recorded and raised with the architect or contract administrator, who will in turn consult with the client to resolve the situation. The consequences of the problem will be brought up at the next site meeting.

Good site managers will request information well in advance of actually needing it on an RFI (request for information) sheet, with dates for when they require the answer. When they are given verbal instructions either by telephone or on site, these will be recorded on a CVI (confirmation of verbal instruction) sheet.

It is not unusual to end up with many RFIs and CVIs, as it is unlikely that all potential problems have been taken into account, particularly on older properties, as explained in Chapter 2.

### Foreman

The site foreman would normally have a 'hands-on' role and carry out physical work, but would also be expected to make decisions affecting the work and would coordinate the operations on site, including the ordering of material, etc.

The foreman would usually be instructed by his head office in matters of the specification of work, and as such would not be expected to act on information from the client, unless he has been given the training and responsibility to record and communicate any changes or revisions to the specification.

Some companies may have different titles for their personnel on site and may refer to a person who is managing a site and not working himself, as a site foreman. The difference between a site foreman and a site manager lies in the level of responsibility for decision-making, and therefore a person's title may not describe their role accurately.

### Subcontractor

The subcontractor would normally be on a fixed price to the builder for his specific area of work, i.e. roof tiling, ceramic tiling, central heating, electrics, etc. Subcontractors will not usually carry out any changes to the specification which affect their work without prior instruction from the main contractor.

Due to the uncertainty of the construction industry with regard to continuity of work, many builders will employ individuals who are effectively subcontractors. However, if they are supplying labour only on a daily rate, it is widely accepted that they work for the builder as an employee.

**Suppliers**

The main contractor would normally supply and install the main building material on projects of a reasonable size as this is a major part of the continuity of any project and is an element where profit is built into his price.

Where you the client are supplying material such as kitchen or bathroom equipment, you must be mindful that if your supplier lets you down and this has an effect on the progress of the project, the builder would have a legitimate claim for extension of time.

These problems can become even worse if the builder is using a subcontractor, for example to install your kitchen. If the allocated time is not achieved due to the material not being available, the builder may also have a claim against you to cover the subcontractor's time lost. This is something that needs to be thought about, and your suppliers will need to see copies of the programme with your order to ensure that they can deliver on time.

If you are considering supplying your own kitchen or bathroom equipment, it is advisable either to have them in your possession prior to the project starting or to have the builder leave the room ready to receive the equipment. You can then organise the labour element once you have the equipment.

Most builders prefer to supply their own material as this is an area where they make a profit on the trade discounts to which they are entitled. Your specification should detail the material and it is worth paying close attention to this as some builders may choose to use an alternative that is inferior to that stated in your specification.

If possible, it is worth obtaining samples of skirting, architrave, tiles and any materials that you know the builder is supplying as detailed in the specification. This will enable you to make comparisons with the material that is eventually brought to site for use on your project.

### Nominated suppliers and subcontractors

Nominated suppliers and subcontractors are those appointed by the client and accepted as part of the construction team by the main contractor. The builder/ contractor takes full responsibility for the nominated suppliers or subcontractors, although he has the right to refuse to instruct them if reasonable grounds exist.

### Health and safety

It is the responsibility of the builder to work in accordance with the Health and Safety at Work Act 1974, and the Management of Health and Safety at Work Regulations 1999. These Acts and Regulations are very comprehensive. However, there are basic duties of care that the builder owes to his employees and anyone who is associated with the project.

A small building company would normally use a health and safety consultant to advise them on their obligations and responsibilities. These are to:

◆ secure the health, safety and welfare of people at work;

◆ protect people other than those at work against risks to their health and safety arising from work activities;

◆ control the keeping and use of explosive or highly flammable or otherwise dangerous substances, and generally prevent people from unlawfully having or using such substances.

If you feel that these obligations are not being adhered to, you must bring it to the attention of the builder/ contractor in order for him to address the problem.

If the problem continues, it is advisable to seek advice from your local health and safety executive.

## THE DESIGN TEAM

### Project manager

On larger projects where a project manager has been appointed the client's main involvement would be at the initial concept stages and in budgeting details. Project management concerns the effective control of projects in land, real estate and construction.

Project managers are responsible for controlling or coordinating the whole development process. Project managers represent their client to ensure increased efficiency, economy, communication and successful completion of projects based on the original client brief.

There are different fee structures that can be used, such as a lump sum price or a percentage of the overall spend. The latter would normally be put in place where there are likely to be changes in the specification due to circumstances such as unknown ground conditions or if structural elements need to be calculated as the project proceeds.

### Architect/architectural technologist

These are specialists in building design and construction techniques. The training for both is similar in many respects, the difference being that architects specialise in concept design issues while technologists specialise in construction and technology. Traditionally appointed as lead consultant or project leader, they may be involved from inception through to completion on larger projects.

### Chartered surveyors

Chartered surveyors cover a diverse range of specialist activities dealing with land, property and development. Below are just a few of the specialist areas.

*Building surveying*

Building surveying is one of the widest areas of practice. Chartered building surveyors cover all aspects of property and construction from supervising multi-million pound projects to planning domestic extensions.

Building surveyors are experts in investigating problems, diagnosing and remedying defects, and advising on possible consequences and alternative solutions.

*Commercial property surveyor*

The work of a chartered surveyor in this area covers all types of real estate used for business purposes. Professional services cover the following:

◆ purchase, sale and leasing of real estate;

- management (of all resources including both human and financial);

- landlord and tenant;

- corporate real estate;

- telecommunications;

- valuations;

- investment (advice for investment appraisal, etc.);

- development and planning;

- real estate finance and funding.

*Residential surveyor*

The work of a chartered surveyor in this area covers all types of real estate used for residential purposes. Professional services include:

- agency purchase, sale and leasing of residential real estate;

- management of public and private residential property;

- landlord and tenant;

- valuation and survey of residential property;

- investment (advice for investment appraisal, etc.);

- development and planning.

*Quantity surveyor*

The quantity surveyor may be appointed at an early stage in a project to advise the client and design team of construction costs and procurement methods.

On larger projects where a bill of quantities is required, the quantity surveyor will undertake the measuring and scheduling of the building materials to enable the contractors to price accurately. A bill of quantities is a document which details fairly accurately the amount of materials that will be used on the project. The quantity surveyor may also prepare tender packages consisting of contracts and documentation, and also provide cost control by way of valuations and certification of payments to the contractor during the construction phase.

**Structural engineer**

A structural engineer will advise on structural solutions to building designs. He may advise and calculate the size of structural components and foundations, etc. Generally, the stability of the structure is his responsibility and he will provide all calculations and details to the local authority for approval as necessary.

**Environment and other service engineers (mechanical and electrical consultants, etc.)**

In designing modern structures, many building, environment and other services such as heating and air conditioning, need to be considered. The services consultant will provide design solutions (layout drawings, specifications, etc.) to accompany the architectural design and tender packages. Their work may include the following:

- plumbing (hot and cold water supplies);
- heating;
- lighting;
- ventilation (natural and mechanical, air conditioning);
- acoustics;
- sanitation;
- communications (lifts, escalators, etc.);
- telecommunications;
- air conditioning.

### Party wall surveyors (all types of projects)

Party wall surveyors are specialists providing advice and services relating to the Party Wall Act 1996. The Act provides a framework for preventing and resolving disputes in relation to alterations and extensions near neighbouring buildings.

### Facilities management (large organisations)

Facilities management is the total management of all services to support the core business of an organisation. Using 'space planning', the facilities manager can implement office relocations of any size and complexity.

Facilities managers will look at the best use of space, and find suitable technology solutions, human resources and safe surroundings. Consideration will be given to legal responsibilities such as health and safety, fire protection and escape, access and security.

## WHAT IF THINGS GO WRONG?

Unfortunately things do go wrong in all industries and there are far too many scenarios to list, however with the correct planning and understanding of the issues these can be minimised.

By taking the time to read and/or discuss the issues with the appropriate people, you can and will become more confident in your decision making. The most important decision that needs to be made is employing the right person or firm in the first place.

In addition to talking to friends who may be able to recommend a reliable contractor or builder there is a scheme available on the Internet that has been set up to address the issue head on.

TrustMark is an award-winning scheme supported by the Government, consumer groups and building industry to help you find reputable firms to do repair, maintenance and improvement work inside and outside your home.

TrustMark have approved, and brought together under one umbrella, trade associations and other certification organisations that have strict criteria for ensuring that its members meet certain standards that the Government has set.

If a firm displays the TrustMark logo, you are safe in the knowledge that a set of minimum standards have been met, including:

+ A TrustMark approved scheme operator has checked the firm's technical skills, trading record and financial position;
+ The firm has signed up to a code of practice that includes insurance, good health and safety practices and customer care;
+ The approved scheme operator has checked and will continue to monitor their quality of work, trading practices and customer satisfaction;
+ The firm will tell you about any building regulations you must meet and may be able to give you the certificates you need;
+ If you have a problem or disagreement with the firm, there will be a clear and user-friendly complaints

procedure to try to help sort out the problem;

- If the firm doesn't automatically provide insurance cover you will have the option to buy a warranty in case it goes out of business.

TrustMark is growing fast and has attracted through its approved scheme many thousands of reputable firms covering all the trades for work inside and outside your home.

- Federation of Master Builders (FMB) MasterBond scheme
- Glass and Glazing Federation (GGF)
- Dulux Select Decorators (Dulux)
- Heating and Ventilation Contractors Association (HVCA)
- National Association of Professional Inspectors & Testers (NAPIT)
- National Inspection Council for Electrical Installation Contracting (NICEIC)
- Electrical Contractors Association (ECA)
- National Federation of Roofing Contractors (NFRC)
- Lead Contractors Association (LCA)
- Association of Professional Landscapers (APL)

You can contact TrustMark on their website at www.trustmark.orq.uk

Please note that TrustMark does not offer a telephone advice service. Everything you need to know should be available on their website.

In the event that things do go wrong and despite your best efforts the situation is deteriorating, stop the work, discuss the problems with the owner of the firm, or the contractor directly and give them the opportunity to rectify the problem.

If you are still not satisfied, contact your legal advisor and employ the services of a professional Adjudicator. Avoid getting into a confrontational situation and always date and document everything that is said and take photographic evidence where appropriate.

# Index

# If you want to know how ... to build your own home

More and more people are setting out to build their own dream home. This book will help you turn your dream into reality by explaining the process, stage-by-stage.

'Here you will find the practical knowledge required to go beyond your aspirations, to take that first step and start building the perfect home. At the end of the day, you will acquire the home you want, rather than one forced upon you from a limited variety, designed and constructed by a builder whose only motivation is to profit from your purchase. Instead of having to fit into a house, you can finally make a house fit you!'

*Tony Booth and Mike Dyson*

**How to Build Your Own Home**
The ultimate guide to managing a self-build project and creating your dream house
*Tony Booth and Mike Dyson*

This book will guide you through the fundamental elements of the self-build programme, from identifying and assessing a suitable building-plot to arranging finance and contractors. It deals with architects and designers, surveyors, labourers and tradesmen. It explains how to obtain planning permission and where to find appropriate insurance protection whilst construction is underway. Essentially, this book provides you with the know-how you need to complete a successful self-build project.

**ISBN 978 1 84528 192 2**

# If you want to know how ... to keep your home and your family safe from crime

'There is a lot that the average person can do to protect themselves, their family and their property. This book will teach you how to perform a security review on your home and show you what countermeasures you can take to ensure that you are *highly unlikely* to be a victim of crime.'

*Des Conway*

**The Home Security Handbook**
How to keep your home and family safe from crime
*D. G. Conway*

Surveys have revealed that when asked what people worry most about for themselves and their family 45% of them said 'CRIME'. Crime statistics certainly indicate that people have good reason to worry: A burglary takes place on average every 30 seconds in the UK.

Alarming though this and other statistics may be, this book will show you how you can use them to reduce the risk of becoming a crime statistic yourself. It will teach you how to audit and review your home and lifestyle, to identify a range of vulnerabilities, threats and risks and then show you how to provide effective countermeasures to avoid the threat and reduce the risk.

The countermeasures suggested are designed to be realistic, achievable at minimal cost and effort and simple enough to be introduced or implemented by the average person.

Des Conway has over 20 years security experience, which combines police service with commercial security consultancy. He has experienced countless security reviews of domestic and commercial properties, delivering reports highlighting vulnerabilities, and recommending simple, affordable and achievable countermeasures.

ISBN 978 1 84528 024 6

# If you want to know how . . . to be a property millionaire

TV star Annie Hulley has amassed a substantial property portfolio in just three years. In this book she explains how she achieved it, the mistakes she made along the way, and what she's gleaned from the experience.

'I now have a substantial investment property portfolio and that is the reason for writing this book, to show that from humble beginnings you too can achieve your goal of being a property millionaire.'

*Annie Hulley*

**How to be a Property Millionaire**
From Coronation Street to Canary Wharf
*Annie Hulley*

'A must-read book . . . a practical guide for anyone who has an interest in investing in bricks and mortar.' – *OPP*

'. . . loads of advice on getting on the property ladder in the UK, plus a section on holiday lets and second homes . . . and a chapter with advice on buying in foreign markets.' – *Homes Worldwide*

'Hulley's guide covers a huge range of subjects relating to buying property, including different types of mortgages, buying at auctions, buying off plan, tax liabilities, estate agents, holiday homes and much more. She's done her homework.' – *Observer*

**ISBN 978 1 85703 857 6**

# If you want to know how ... to make your first property purchase a success

'The sense of achievement gained from buying a first property is tremendous. It is a momentous occasion, filled with pride and contentment.

'It is true that there is a growing trend and an ever expanding ability to buy property, but there is associated with it a mountainous capacity for critical mistakes. This book is intended for savvy investors who wish to evade such errors. By following the advice laid out in this book, conducting a thorough personal assessment, investigating properties worthy of purchase and exploring all the alternatives, you will find yourself able to buy a dwelling that meets your needs and one that provides financial security for the future.'

*Tony Booth*

**The Beginner's Guide to Property Investment**
The ultimate handbook for first-time buyers and would-be property investors
*Tony Booth*

This book provides an insight into many key issues; it explains what constitutes a sound investment, how you can examine your borrowing potential and create a golden credit rating, what mortgages are available and which are most suitable. It also discusses alternative property investment; buy-to-let, let-to-buy, renovation, buying property abroad, self-build and self-employed business enterprise; and shares generous amounts of inside information and well-kept trade secrets.

**ISBN 978 1 85703 961 0**

**If you want to know how** ... to manage a successful buy-to-let enterprise

'By empowering yourself with the information in this book, you will enjoy the financial and personal rewards that becoming a landlord can provide. You will also have the satisfaction of knowing that you are in full control of your most valued asset. The private rented sector is an exciting, stimulating and challenging arena for novice and professional alike; this book will guide you through its many facets and show you how to generate a considerable income.'

*Tony Booth*

**The Buy to Let Handbook**
How to invest for profit in residential property and manage the letting yourself
*Tony Booth*

'An excellent first purchase for anyone contemplating investing in the buy to let market whether they are proposing to manage the property themselves or to use an agent to do it for them. First class and good value for money.' – *The Letting Centre* (*Letting Update Journal*)

'An excellent piece of work that clearly and concisely encapsulates the fundamental issues ... I will be seeking that the book is placed high on recommended reading lists.' – *Philip R Gibbs, Life President of the Residential Landlords Association*

**ISBN 978 1 84528 102 3**

How To Books are available through all good bookshops, or you can order direct from us through Grantham Book Services.

Tel: +44 (0)1476 541080
Fax: +44 (0)1476 541061
Email: orders@gbs.tbs-ltd.co.uk

Or via our website

www.howtobooks.co.uk

To order via any of these methods please quote the title(s) of the book(s) and your credit card number together with its expiry date.

For further information about our books and catalogue, please contact:

How To Books
Spring Hill House
Spring Hill Road
Begbroke
Oxford OX5 1RX

Visit our web site at

www.howtobooks.co.uk

Or you can contact us by email at info@howtobooks.co.uk